THE RHETORIC OF
THE CIVIL-RIGHTS MOVEMENT

ISSUES and SPOKESMEN SERIES

A RANDOM HOUSE STUDY IN SPEECH

GENERAL EDITOR | Don Geiger | *University of California, Berkeley*

HAIG A. BOSMAJIAN
University of Washington

HAMIDA BOSMAJIAN
Seattle University

THE
RHETORIC
of ——————————————
THE
CIVIL-RIGHTS
MOVEMENT

Random House
NEW YORK

ACKNOWLEDGMENTS

The authors acknowledge their appreciation to reprint material contained
herein to the following:

Quotation from Martin Luther King, Jr., *Where Do We Go From Here:
Chaos or Community?*, Copyright © 1967 by Martin Luther King, Jr.
Reprinted by permission of Harper & Row, Publishers.

Martin Luther King, Jr., "Letter from Birmingham City Jail," is reprinted by permission of Joan Daves, Copyright © 1963 by Martin Luther
King, Jr.

"A Debate at Cornell University," reprinted by permission of Cornell
United Religious Work, from *Dialogue*, II (May 1962), pp. 13–18.

"Keynote Address to the NAACP Annual Convention," reprinted by permission of Roy Wilkins.

"Power and Racism," reprinted by permission of the Student Nonviolent
Coordinating Committee (SNCC).

"Speech at Morgan State College," reprinted by permission of the Student
Nonviolent Coordinating Committee (SNCC).

"Speech at the National Conference on Black Power," reprinted by permission of the Congress of Racial Equality (CORE).

N 1 0 6

The *Issues and Spokesmen Series* has been developed as a response to a need widely expressed in the areas of rhetoric and public address: in public speaking and written composition, in speech fundamentals, discussion, argumentation, and persuasion, and in rhetorical, political, and social criticism. Broadly, instructors and students of these matters desire an enriched rhetorical substance to complement the prevailing emphasis on method and general principles.

What is particularly needed, we agree in department meetings and at conventions, are more collections of speeches and writings focused on a significant theme or problem; or we search for concrete models of excellent persuasion and argument in connection with questions truly relevant to our students' increasingly active interest in "participatory" democracy; or we want materials that will encourage depth and range in critical analysis of particular problems, as we also wish for more studies designed to excite students to independent research; or we seek striking illustrations of the ways in which speakers and writers strive to effect politically and socially consequential attitudes and decisions. These are the kinds of material that the Random House series of books on *Issues and Spokesmen* will help to supply.

Certainly I do not suggest that these books will exhaust our educational need for speeches and writings that mean business in the realm of public affairs, or that they are our only available resources. My more sober aim, having identified the *Issues and Spokesmen* books as essays in provisioning rhetoric with appropriate substance, is to describe briefly the general design and pattern of this group of books.

The term "Issues" in the series title is best understood in the popular sense of "matter the decision of which is of special or public importance," and each book focuses on a significant controversy or question of public policy. Thus each volume contains a selection by its author-editor of speeches, or speeches and writings, by important spokesmen organized around an issue of major contemporary importance or importance to its time and clear relevance to our own. Each book also contains its author-editor's fairly long essay, covering all or some of such matters as the social, political, and intellectual environment of the issue; the background of the issue in history and rhetorical tradition; a description of the careers and roles of the spokesmen involved; or an account of the rhetorical techniques and the principles of analysis with which the student will be concerned as he becomes familiar with the issue and re-examines the speeches and writings. Speeches are presented chronologically and, wherever possible, in their entirety.

Headnotes and footnotes serve familiar functions—identifying speakers, the immediate occasion of a given speech, allusions requiring explanation, and the like. In addition, special interrogative footnotes draw the student more thoughtfully into the speech—its language, line of argument, and techniques. Questions and comments in these footnotes are not intended to pre-empt the student's own critical focus. Rather, they will serve as suggestive examples of what perceptive critics notice and question when analyzing a text. Broader implications of the speeches and writings are considered in each volume's section for inquiry and bibliography. The latter material serves as an inductive guide to students' further examination and discussion of a given issue.

Since my purpose is to comment generally, I shall say little about that which is nonetheless the most important aspect of the series, the individuality of the separate works. Each of these books bears the distinctive stamp of its editor or co-editors; and each book represents an independent interest in substance and approach, as in toto the volumes reflect the common interests of expert students of the rhetoric of public affairs. I think that many other readers will share my admiration for the workmanship of the individual authors of these volumes and take pleasure in their educational contributions.

Don Geiger

CONTENTS

THE RHETORIC OF
THE CIVIL-RIGHTS MOVEMENT

Introduction

On Thursday, December 1, 1955, in Montgomery, Alabama, Mrs. Rosa Parks, a Negro seamstress in her early forties, was on her way home after a tiring day's work at a department store. Mrs. Parks boarded her bus and sat in the first seat behind the white section; that is, she sat in the first row of seats designated for Negroes. After she sat down, the bus driver ordered her and three other Negro passengers to give up their seats to four white passengers who had boarded the bus. Because all the seats were taken by this time, Mrs. Parks would have had to stand while a white male passenger took the seat she was ordered to vacate. The three other Negroes complied with the driver's order, but Mrs. Parks quietly refused and remained where she sat. The police were called; she was taken off the bus and charged for her action of violating the transportation segregation law of Montgomery, Alabama.

Mrs. Parks had no way of knowing then that her action and arrest were to be precipitating factors of a Negro protest, a civil-rights movement, and a bus boycott that was to last over a year. Her action and the subsequent Montgomery bus boycott, however, were the beginnings of a civil-rights movement which up to that time had not sustained itself. Several writers and civil-rights leaders, black and white, have pointed to Mrs. Parks' actions and the resulting boycott as the beginning of the civil-rights movement that evolved during the decade that followed. Martin Luther King, Jr., writing in 1958 about the first day of the boycott, said: "That night [December 5, 1955] we were starting a movement that would gain national recognition; whose echoes would ring in the ears of people of every nation; a movement that would astound the oppressor, and bring new hope to the oppressed." [1] Louis E. Lomax wrote that "the Negro

revolt is properly dated from the moment Mrs. Parks said 'No'
to the bus driver's demand that she get up and let a white man
have her seat." [2] Lerone Bennett, Jr., saw the boycott as the
beginning of a new movement: "The one-day boycott stretched
out to 385 days; the 385 days changed the face and heart of
Negro America, creating a new idea and a new movement that
raced across the South." [3] After enumerating the injustices, indignities, and acts of violence heaped upon the Negro in America for the past one hundred years, Roland T. Heacock asserted:

At last, we became tired (like Rosa Parks) of giving up our seat.
Until the outbreak of these demonstrations in 1956, the year of the
Montgomery bus boycott (and of Mrs. Parks' getting tired) it must
be admitted that with only a few exceptions . . . the majority of
whites in the United States were either ignorant of, or indifferent
to what had been happening to us Negroes.[4]

Arthur Waskow, writing about the four Negro college students who sat down at a Woolworth's lunch counter in Greens-
boro, North Carolina, on February 1, 1960, and who thereby
became the inspiration for subsequent sit-ins, stated that "two
major events the previous decade had helped bring the students
to the point of action"; one was the 1954 decision by the United
States Supreme Court ordering the desegregation of public
schools; the other event that inspired the sit-ins was the Negro
boycott of segregated buses in Montgomery.[5]

As James H. Laue pointed out:

. . . sporadic protests against racism in America have been going
on since the first Africans jumped overboard rather than be sold
into slavery some 400 years ago. But not until the Montgomery bus
boycott and its catapulting of Dr. Martin Luther King, Jr. into
nationwide prominence was the final groundwork laid for development of a widespread desegregation movement. Montgomery dra-
matically showed Negroes a new technique—nonviolent direct action—which had won immediate gains in a hard-core segregationist
area of the Deep South.[6]

After 1957, a sustained series of verbal pronouncements and
physical confrontations by Negroes and their white allies was
brought to bear to persuade Negroes and whites that it was now

time for both to act to bring about equality and justice in a segregated and unjust society. After 1957 came the sit-ins, freedom rides, picketing, mass meetings, and civil-rights marches; protests against segregation in public places took the form of kneel-ins in churches, wade-ins at beaches and swimming pools, and read-ins in public libraries; the jail-in demonstrated that the Negro was not afraid to go to jail to attain his rights as a citizen of the United States. The civil-rights movement brought with it not only these acts of "creative dissent," these "controlled creative disorders," but also a great increase in speech-making and pamphleteering by Negro civil-rights leaders and organizations. Speeches, pamphlets, protest songs, like the physical confrontations, had a rhetorical or suasory function.

The civil-rights leaders faced a formidable rhetorical problem; several questions about their persuasion had to be answered: To whom was their persuasion to be directed? Segregationists? Moderate whites? Negroes? What form should the protest take? What effect would the persuasion have on the audience? For example, on one hand the Montgomery bus boycott was directed against city authorities and the bus company with their segregation policies; yet, on the other hand, the boycott, with the accompanying mass meetings, speeches, songs, and demonstrations, had a persuasive effect upon the thousands of Negroes who had to become united participants in the boycott; unless the Negroes of Montgomery could be persuaded to stop riding the buses, the boycott was doomed to failure. Further, because the nation and the entire world had their attention focused on Montgomery and the actions of the civil-rights leaders, this larger audience also had to be considered, for they too were watching and being persuaded.

The selections in this book constitute some of the verbal persuasion that took place during the decade following the Montgomery bus boycott. The various spokesmen represented here reflect various persuasions. The purpose of this introduction is to present these selections within a rhetorical and historical context. This is not intended as a rhetorical analysis of the various pieces of verbal persuasion; such analysis is the student's task. The questions and exercises at the end of each selection will guide the student in his own rhetorical analysis of the persuasion of the civil-rights movement.

For a decade, through their verbal and nonverbal creative dissent, Negroes were attempting to persuade the American people, in and out of government, that the Negro people could no longer be expected to accept passively the poor housing, poor education, poor representation, poor jobs, and poor health services they had been receiving for the past century as American citizens living in a land of plenty. The statistics showing what white America had done to the Negroes apparently had not persuaded other Americans to give Negroes equal rights and opportunities. The statistics were there for all to see: In March 1966, the Department of Labor announced that nonwhite workers constituted only 11 percent of the civilian labor force but accounted for over 21 percent of the unemployed and 25 percent of the long-term unemployed; in the summer of 1965, the unemployment rate among Negro youths *rose* from 27 percent to 32 percent, while that for white youths *dropped* from 19 percent to 14 percent; the Department of Labor announced that in 1964 the average family income among nonwhites was 56 percent of that among whites; among Negroes, 37 percent of the families had annual incomes below the poverty level of $3,000; the armed services revealed a failure rate of 67.5 percent for Negroes as against 18.8 percent for whites; in 1962, the Census Bureau reported that 80 percent of Negroes with only a grade-school education held unskilled jobs as laborers, porters, and so forth, compared to 50 percent of the whites with similar education; the Census Bureau also reported that 60 percent of Negro high-school graduates were laborers compared to 30 percent of white graduates.

In June 1963, President John F. Kennedy told his nationwide radio and television audience:

The Negro baby in America today, regardless of the section of the nation in which he is born, has about one half as much chance of completing high school as a white baby born in the same place on the same day, one third as much chance of completing college, one third as much chance of becoming a professional man, twice as much chance of becoming unemployed, about one seventh as much chance of earning $10,000 a year, a life expectancy which is seven years shorter, and the prospect of earning only half as much.

Such statistics, however, had little persuasive effect on the white people of America; white America continued to ignore the "invisible man," the Negro.

Through their creative dissent, Negroes went beyond the use of facts and statistics to persuade the American people that the Negro was tired of moving to the back of the bus, tired of seeing his undernourished children receiving second-rate educations, tired of watching whites who murdered and mutilated Negroes set free by southern judges and white juries, tired of being refused service in a segregated restaurant. Through their dissent, Negroes were saying and singing: "We Shall Overcome," "We Shall Not Be Moved," "Ain't Gonna Let Nobody Turn Me Round," "We'll Never Turn Back," "Move on Over or We'll Move on Over You." Through his acts of creative dissent and his verbal pronouncements, the Negro was speaking to all Americans, to local, state, and federal legislators, to the President. This persuasion, however, necessarily also had to be directed to the Negro people themselves who needed to be united, awakened, persuaded, moved to action; civil-rights leaders found that a persuasion that appealed to young Negroes did not necessarily appeal to older Negroes; some militant Negroes preferred more direct action than the creative dissent of the nonviolent demonstrators; such slogans as "black power" came to mean one thing to whites and something else to Negroes; "Move on Over or We'll Move on Over You," directed to white America, became more meaningful to some Negroes than "We Shall Overcome." The rhetorical function and effectiveness of picketing or the mass demonstration or the sit-in or verbal discourse varied with each different audience.

Several civil-rights leaders have commented on the rhetorical function of civil-rights demonstrations, from sit-ins to boycotts, from marching to freedom rides. Writing of the persuasiveness of nonviolent action, Martin Luther King, Jr., said in 1958:

Nonviolence can touch men where the law cannot reach them. When the law regulates behavior it plays an indirect part in molding public sentiment. The enforcement of the law is itself a form of peaceful persuasion. But the law needs help. The courts can order desegregation of the public schools. But what can be done to mitigate the fears, to disperse the hatred, violence, and irrationality gathered around school integration, to take the initiative out of the hands of racial demagogues, to release respect for the law? In the end, for laws to be obeyed, men must believe they are right.

Here nonviolence comes in as the ultimate form of persuasion. It is the method which seeks to implement the just law by appealing to the conscience of the great decent majority who through blindness, fear, pride, or irrationality have allowed their consciences to sleep.

The nonviolent resisters can summarize their message in the following simple terms: We will take direct action against injustice without waiting for other agencies to act. We will not obey unjust laws or submit to unjust practices. We will do this peacefully, openly, cheerfully because our aim is to persuade. We adopt the means of nonviolence because our end is a community at peace with itself. *We will try to persuade with our words, but if our words fail, we will try to persuade with our acts* [italics added].[7]

Until the Montgomery bus boycott, Americans generally had not listened to the words of Negroes asking for the equal rights and opportunities, the equal justice that should have been theirs without the asking. For all intents and purposes, the ears of Americans were shut to the voice of reason when it came to giving the Negro what was supposedly guaranteed to him under the United States Constitution and promised by the American credo.

Roy Wilkins of the NAACP (National Association for the Advancement of Colored People), like King, has recognized the rhetorical function of nonviolent protest demonstrations. Wilkins wrote in 1964 that the Montgomery bus boycott

forced the world to focus on the Negro's condition in the American South. . . . This type of demonstration acts as a powerful persuasive upon the national conscience, especially so in race relations where the merest schoolboy knows the Negro has been grievously mistreated. It exhibits a courage in the face of psychological and physical threats, a willingness to suffer to attain a goal. It is not arrogant. It is peaceful and resolutely righteous. It is a moral and spiritual crusade as disturbingly relentless in its quiet pressure as any bomb or brick.[8]

Not only have civil-rights leaders looked upon their creative dissent as functioning rhetorically, but so have justices on the United States Supreme Court. The rhetorical function of the sit-ins was not missed by the court in *Garner v. Louisiana*; referring to the petitioners, Negroes who had participated in sit-ins at lunch counters, Justice John Marshall Harlan wrote

. . . there was more to the conduct of those petitioners than a bare desire to remain at the "white" lunch counter and their refusal of a police request to move from the counter. We would surely have to be blind not to recognize that petitioners were sitting at these counters, where they knew they would not be served, in order to demonstrate that their race was being segregated in dining facilities in this part of the country.

[Justice Harlan then went on to compare the sit-in demonstration with speech, citing Supreme Court decisions to illustrate and support his position; the sit-in being considered in the Garner case, he said, is] as much a part of the "free trade of ideas," *Abrams v. United States*, 250 U.S. 616, 630 (Holmes, Jr., dissenting), as is verbal expression, more commonly thought of as "speech." It, like speech, appeals to good sense and to "the power of reason as applied through public discussion," *Whitney v. California*, 274 U.S. 357, 375 (Brandeis, J., concurring), just as much as, if not more than, a public oration delivered from a soapbox at a street corner. This court has never limited the right to speak, a protected "liberty" under the Fourteenth Amendment, *Gitlow v. New York*, 268 U.S. 652, 666, to mere verbal expression. . . . If the act of displaying a red flag as a symbol of opposition to organized government is a liberty encompassed within free speech as protected by the Fourteenth Amendment, *Stromberg v. California* . . . the act of sitting at a privately owned lunch counter with the consent of the owner, as a demonstration of opposition to enforced segregation, is surely within the same range of protection.[9]

The rhetorical function of the sit-ins and other acts of creative dissent has been carefully considered by Harry Kalven, Jr., professor of law at the University of Chicago. His views related to Justice Harlan's concurring opinion in *Garner v. Louisiana* and the persuasiveness of the demonstration are expressed most lucidly in a lecture entitled "Trespass and the First Amendment" delivered in 1964 at Ohio State University. In the lecture Professor Kalven stated:

As a sociological perception, it seems to me Justice Harlan's characterization of the protest as a First Amendment activity rings true. Certainly the sit-in ceremony, and the South's response to it, have been sensationally successful in making the Negro grievance known, not simply to the Negro community, but to the entire country. And not so much known as felt. The rhetoric of the silent waiting has been extraordinarily good; there cannot be ways of making a point as well with words; and finally, to borrow a point that the Court has been eloquent about in leaflet cases, we have again here a problem of the poor man's printing press. The sit-in gesture gives a powerful resource to the Negro community, which does not have great communication resources. In the end, the wisdom and restraint that has, by and large thus far, held the Negro self-help tactic to these gestures as passive, patient, peaceful protest has not only been effective rhetoric but has been the circumstance making it possible and plausible to characterize it as First Amendment activity.[10]

The persuasiveness and the rhetorical function of the acts of creative dissent have also been recognized by the legal scholar Milton R. Konvitz who has observed that there are times when

. . . the authorities and the public simply would not hear the spoken word. When people will not listen, men with grievances must find another way of exercising their right of petition for redress of grievances. [Konvitz uses the 1965 Selma, Alabama, march to illustrate his point; it was Selma where] 13,000 whites disfranchised 15,000 Negroes, and where the sheriff, James G. Clark, and his helmeted posse terrorized the Negro community; but no one paid attention until the Negroes, led by Martin Luther King, Jr., marched and demonstrated, and 3,400 Negroes, including Dr. King, were put in jail, and 165 Negro youths were taken on a forced march by Sheriff Clark and his deputies with night sticks and electric cattle prods. Then, and only then, did the rest of the nation listen, and only then did the President of the United States strongly denounce infringement of voting rights and pledge vigorous legal action, and state that he would ask Congress for new legislation to eliminate barriers to the right to vote.[11]

The President and the nation, previously hesitant about acting upon the grievances of the Negroes, were now persuaded to act after the news media had revealed nationally and internationally the inhumanity and prejudice and brutality in contrast to the human dignity of creative dissent.

The rhetorical function of civil-rights demonstrations has been recognized not only by civil-rights leaders, Supreme Court justices, and legal scholars but also by scholars in other areas of study. Political scientists Donald Matthews and James Prothro wrote in 1966: "The demonstrations were a classic example of propaganda of the deed. We must judge the efficacy of the sit-ins and the freedom rides primarily by their effect on public opinion." [12] Professor Franklyn Haiman, chairman of the Department of Public Address and Group Communication at Northwestern University, writing about the rhetoric of the streets, uses the term "rhetoric" in its widest sense in analyzing the rhetorical function and legality of such demonstrations as sit-ins, marches, and picketing. Haiman recognizes that some of the activities he discusses fall within the purview of rhetoric only if the term is used in a broader sense than it has been in the past. Traditionally, Aristotle's definition of rhetoric as the art of discovering all the available means of persuasion in any given case has been applied to verbal communication. If we take Aristotle's phrase to mean literally "all the available means of persuasion," writes Haiman, "then we do have here a problem in rhetorical criticism." [13]

In examining the rhetoric of the civil-rights movement, one must use the term "rhetoric" in its broadest sense: it must include both the verbal and nonverbal symbols of persuasion. As

Martin Luther King, Jr., put it, "We will try to persuade with our words, but if our words fail, we will try to persuade with our acts." Through verbal persuasion the civil-rights speaker or writer attempts to convey his message, to communicate with his audience; he attempts to arouse in the individuals in his audience a sense of involvement and participation; he attempts to create, perhaps, a sense of unity and belonging. Individuals who are not moved by the orator's words, however, may derive from the demonstration the sense of the demonstrator's message, the feeling of unity, belonging, and involvement; the non-verbal rhetorical act of marching or picketing may communicate, may get people to act where the verbal communication did not. Participating in a mass march can give the participant an identity he did not possess outside the demonstration; social unification, a unification that could not be achieved through verbal persuasion, can be achieved through the march; the participant's importance is magnified by seeing himself a hundred or a thousandfold. The persuasiveness of a march or parade has been observed by Leonard Doob who writes that

. . . the parader and also the bystander unavoidably perceives that many, many people are being moved by that cause and so they, too, will have a tendency to lend their support. [As the demonstration takes place before him] the individual may come to a hasty decision (he will join the navy, buy a bond, enroll in a party, sign a code, etc.) which may be contrary to other attitudes within him that have remained latent during that decision. The decision, however, if not the attitude which has brought it about, may be more permanent as a result of the binding character of social contacts.[14]

The civil-rights marches gave participants, and some observers, an opportunity to communicate their grievances, an opportunity that would not have been open to them if communication were limited to verbal persuasion. Participants, and some observers, exchanged anonymity for identity; strength, solidarity, and commitment prevailed where weakness, indecision, and passivity existed before. Arthur Waskow observes:

In advancing voter registration among Negroes who had previously been too cowed, too hopeless, or too ignorant of the law to try to register, the movement began more and more to use mass public marches. These were a useful technique for mobilizing Negro strength, destroying the old white images of Negro passivity, demonstrating Negro solidarity both to the Negroes themselves and to local white power structures, and attracting national attention both to their old plight and their new militance.[15]

Looking back over the 1957–1967 decade of civil-rights marches, mass meetings, sit-ins, and other nonverbal symbols of persuasion, one can see how they functioned rhetorically, in some cases with some success. At the same time, however, one must recognize that what at the moment appeared as success turned out in the long run to be ineffectual in bringing about changes in the political, social, and economic condition of the Negroes in America. Enthusiastic, well-attended demonstrations often gave the immediate impression of accomplishment, yet in the end little long-range persuasion took place. Demonstrations that were looked upon as ends in themselves turned out to be weak means of attaining significant change. An intrinsic danger of marches and demonstrations is that the participants deceive themselves into believing, after having marched and having demonstrated, that they have accomplished something to bring about change. The limits of mass demonstrations were made clear in 1961 when protest marches and demonstrations in Albany, Georgia, brought no tangible successes. Observing that Albany was a "staggering defeat" for Martin Luther King, Jr., and the freedom movement, Lerone Bennett, Jr., has stated that the "sit-ins and Freedom rides had given men excessive confidence in the power of demonstrations, which are, in truth, useful instruments if used in the right place and within the right strategic framework." [16]

The first two selections in this book are directly associated with historic civil-rights demonstrations in April 1963: the Birmingham demonstrations. The April 16 public letter from the Birmingham jail by Martin Luther King, Jr., was written while he was imprisoned for his participation in a civil-rights march through Birmingham, Alabama. Both the demonstrations and the verbal documents constituted persuasive efforts by civil-rights leaders and speakers. King commented on the effectiveness of the Birmingham demonstrations and the impact they had on the Negro:

When legal contests were the sole form of activity, the ordinary Negro was involved as a passive spectator. His interest was stirred, but his energies were unemployed. Mass marches transformed the common man into the star performer and engaged him in a total commitment. Yet nonviolent resistance caused no explosions of anger—it instigated no riots—it controlled anger and released it under discipline for maximum effect. What lobbying and imploring could not do in legislative halls, marching feet accomplished a thousand miles away. When the Southern Christian Leadership Conference went into Birmingham in 1963, it intended to change that city. But the effect of its campaign was so extensive that President Kennedy was forced to conclude that national legislation was indispensable, and the first civil rights bill with substance was enacted in 1964. Nonviolent direct action had proved to be the most effective generator of change that the movement had seen, and by 1965 all civil rights organizations had embraced it as theirs.[17]

For decades, Negroes either had passively accepted their segregated status or had verbally pleaded with white authorities to end job discrimination and segregation in public facilities, but to no avail. The Birmingham demonstrations, marching, picketing, sit-ins, functioned rhetorically to bring about desegregation of lunch counters, rest rooms, waiting rooms, and drinking fountains in department stores and elicited a promise from city leaders to end racial discrimination in employment in some downtown stores. As King pointed out, the demonstrations also had a wider effect; the entire nation reacted, including Congress and the President.

Through the news media the entire nation saw Birmingham police unleashing police dogs upon children and using high-pressure fire hoses against demonstrators. Arthur Waskow has pointed out the national impact of this violence directed against the demonstrators:

On May 4, a notable news photograph appeared all over the world, showing a Birmingham police dog leaping at the throat of a Negro schoolboy. If there was any single event or moment at which the 1960s generation of "new Negroes" can be said to have turned into a major social force, the appearance of that photograph was it. Intense pressure upon President John F. Kennedy to initiate federal action began to be applied the moment that photograph appeared, and both financial and political support for all organizations in the civil rights movement multiplied at once.[18]

The effect of this photograph illustrates the rhetorical function of a picture. Apparently where persuasive speeches and articles and books had not persuaded some Americans to give financial and political support to the civil-rights movement, the visual images of peaceful demonstrators abused by the Birmingham police did bring support.

During the demonstrations, eight Alabama clergymen in Birmingham published a plea in the newspapers urging the Negro community to withdraw support from the civil-rights demonstrations being conducted there: the eight clergymen said that they were "convinced that these demonstrations are unwise and untimely." Their letter appears in this book, followed by the selection, "Letter from Birmingham City Jail," King's answer to the clergymen. King's letter was reprinted in several periodicals and was distributed across the nation in pamphlet form. Since this was a public letter, King was making an attempt to persuade not only the specific eight clergymen but also Americans in general, Negro and white, that the nonviolent civil-rights demonstrations were justified and in keeping with American and Christian principles.

On Good Friday, April 12, 1963, Dr. King, participating in a civil-rights march in Birmingham, was arrested, held incommunicado for twenty-four hours in solitary confinement, and not allowed to see his lawyers during that time. After eight days of imprisonment, King accepted bond and was released. While he was imprisoned, King wrote his letter in answer to the eight clergymen who were critical of the "series of demonstrations by some of our Negro citizens, directed and led in part by outsiders." King said that the letter was written:

under somewhat constricting circumstances. Begun on the margins of the newspaper in which the statement [of the eight clergymen] appeared while I was in jail, the letter was continued on scraps of writing paper supplied by a friendly Negro trusty, and concluded on a pad my attorneys were eventually permitted to leave me.[19]

Considering the time, the place, the audience, the speaker and the form, "Letter from Birmingham City Jail" can stand side by side with the great public letters of the past such as Émile Zola's 1898 letter to the president of the French Republic denouncing the Dreyfus decision and Thomas Mann's 1937 public letter to the dean of the Philosophical Faculty of the University of Bonn. Dr. King has based his arguments on premises that are acceptable to almost all Americans and more particularly to the eight clergymen; he has identified these premises with respected, revered men, from Socrates to Tillich, from Aquinas to Buber. His premises—from laymen and clergymen, Protestants, Catholics, and Jews—contain nothing mean or low or hateful. The validity of his arguments stands up to examination. He has amassed more than enough specifics and examples to make his inductive arguments acceptable. King's use of emotional proofs and his style are not only appropriate for his audience but are also consistent with the man, his philosophy, and his movement. He has reasoned with his audience; he has not insulted them by speaking down to them, nor has he taken the pose of the intellectual superior. While he arouses the emotions, he has not turned to inciting anger or hate, fear or envy. King's letter is rhetorically superior to any specific persuasive discourse that his white critics and adversaries have produced. He has remained on a high plane; his goal for the brotherhood of man is thus exemplified in the word and in the spirit of his "Letter from Birmingham City Jail."

Several months after the Birmingham demonstrations, the

largest civil-rights demonstration the nation had seen up to that time was organized and carried out. In February 1963, A. Philip Randolph, president of the Negro American Labor Council, suggested a plan of mass "pilgrimage" to Washington, D. C., to dramatize job discrimination against Negroes and the "unemployment crisis" among Negroes; James Farmer of the Congress of Racial Equality said that the Washington march should help persuade legislators, who were delaying passage of civil-rights legislation, "of the urgency of the situation." On August 28, 1963, approximately 250,000 people, 40,000 to 50,000 of them whites, marched on Washington. From across the nation came warnings and predictions that the march would result in riots, violence, and bloodshed. Approximately 500 police, national guardsmen, and army reservists were on hand to maintain order. The predictions of disorder and violence never materialized; the massive, orderly demonstration took place without one demonstrator being arrested. President Kennedy said that he had been impressed with the "deep fervor and quiet dignity" that characterized the marchers.

There were differences of opinion on whether the march on Washington was decisive in persuading the President and Congress to speed up civil-rights legislation, but there is little doubt that the demonstrations had other positive effects. Kenneth B. Clark recognized that the march on Washington did not change the everyday lives of the "masses of oppressed Negroes in the Southern states or in the Northern ghettos. The poor housing, the poor schools, job discrimination, and the stigmatized and rejected status which were the lot of the Negro in America in July 1963 remained precisely his predicament in July 1964." [20] But Clark did see the march on Washington as functioning rhetorically in other ways:

Yet the march had a dramatic impact on the morale of middle-class Negroes. For many Negroes in the North, participation in the march was their first decision to assume the risks of action. For many alienated Negroes in the South, it revealed for the first time the extent of support for their cause in the rest of the country. In addition, it may be that the march was not so much an effective instrument of social change—for it probably was not—as an evidence of a consensus of support from respectable middle-class groups, white and Negro, hitherto inarticulate, disorganized, and irresolute. It may have helped to convince some persons in the seats of power that some degree of social change was desirable, if only to contain the energies of protest.[21]

Lerone Bennett, Jr., writes: "As a morale booster, the March was a stunning success. But as an exercise in leadership, it was something less than scintillating. The March was not coordinated with anything that preceded it or anything that followed it. It led nowhere and was not intended to lead anywhere. It was not planned as an event within a coherent plan of action. As a result, the March was a stimulating but detached and isolated episode." [22] Bennett has said that with the march on Washington, the civil-rights "rebellion" became national. Writing in a similar vein, Murray Kempton observed: "If the march was important, it was because it represented an acceptance of the Negro revolt as part of the American myth, and so an acceptance of the revolutionaries into the American establishment." [23]

There were, however, Negroes who saw little to be gained by conducting such demonstrations as the march on Washington and the Birmingham marches and sit-ins. The Washington march was referred to as the "Farce on Washington" by Malcolm X who wrote in his autobiography:

Yes, I was there. I observed that circus. Who ever heard of angry revolutionists all harmonizing "We Shall Overcome . . . Summer Day . . ." while tripping and swaying along arm-in-arm with the very people they were supposed to be angrily revolting against? Who ever heard of angry revolutionists swinging their bare feet together with their oppressor in lilypad park ponds, with gospels and guitars and "I Have A Dream" speeches?

. . .

In a subsequent press poll, not one Congressman or Senator with a previous record of opposition to civil rights said he had changed his views. What did anyone expect? How was a one-day "integrated" picnic going to counter-influence these representatives of prejudice rooted deep in the psyche of the American white man for four hundred years? [24]

In 1964, the speaker of these words, the most articulate of the Black Muslims, broke with his leader, Elijah Muhammad, to organize the Muslim Mosque, Inc., and the nonreligious Organization of Afro-American Unity: Malcolm X was assassinated in New York on February 21, 1965. Before he broke with Elijah Muhammad, Malcolm X delivered scores of speeches and participated in debates defending and explaining the Black Muslim position and denouncing whites and the civil-rights leaders of NAACP, CORE, SNCC (Student Nonviolent Coordinating Committee), and SCLC (Southern Christian Leadership Conference). The Black Muslims were not interested in integrating with the whites; they had no interest in participating in American politics where white man was running against white man. In his Cornell University debate (included here, pp. 59–88) with James Farmer of CORE, Malcolm X stated why the followers of "the honorable Elijah Muhammad don't accept integration"; in this debate he proposed a separation of the races and a suggestion that some of the territory of the United States be set aside to let the Negroes "go off to ourselves and try and solve our own problems."

The Black Muslims' nonparticipation in American politics, as C. Eric Lincoln explains,

has been due partly to their belief that America is already corrupt and doomed, and partly to their sense of futility in electing any white man to office. Malcolm X notes that "Roosevelt promised, Truman promised, Eisenhower promised. Negroes are still knocking on the door begging for civil rights. . . . Do you mean to tell me that in a powerful country like this, a so-called Christian country, that a handful of men from the South can prevent the North, the West, the Central States and the East from giving Negroes the rights the Constitution says they already have? No! I don't believe that and neither do you. No white man really wants the Black Man to have his rights, or he'd have them. The United States does everything else it wants to do." [25]

In his autobiography Malcolm X said that when he was asked during the 1964 presidential campaign whether he favored Lyndon Johnson or Barry Goldwater,

I said I felt that as far as the American black man was concerned they were both just about the same. I felt that it was for the black man only a question of Johnson, the fox, or Goldwater, the wolf. "Conservatism" in America's politics means "Let's keep the niggers in their place." And "liberalism" means "Let's keep the *kneegrows* in their place—but tell them we'll treat them a little better; let's fool them more, with more promises." With these choices, I felt that the American black man only needed to choose which one to be eaten by, the "liberal" fox or the "conservative" wolf—because both of them would eat him.[26]

Malcolm's attitude at that time toward the whites was reflected in a 1962 speech in which he said, referring to an airplane crash that took the lives of over 120 whites (mostly southerners), that God had answered the prayers of the Black Muslims:

He dropped an airplane out of the sky with over a hundred and twenty white people on it, because Muslims believe in an eye for an eye and a tooth for a tooth. He gets rid of one hundred and twenty in one whoop. But thanks to God or Jehovah or Allah, we will continue to pray and we hope that every day another plane falls out of the sky.[27]

What the Black Muslims had to say about civil-rights leaders such as Roy Wilkins, James Farmer, Martin Luther King, Jr., and Thurgood Marshall sounded almost as contemptuous as what the Muslims had to say about the whites. After Thurgood Marshall, one-time chief legal counsel of the NAACP, had denounced the Black Muslims, Malcolm X referred to Marshall as a "twentieth century Uncle Tom" and declared himself "too busy to worry about the envious yapping of every jealous dog that is paid to bark at him." [28] As for Martin Luther King, Jr., and his passive resistance techniques, the Black Muslims opposed both; as C. Eric Lincoln has explained in his analysis of the Black Muslims:

They oppose King because he emphasizes the Christian principles of loving the oppressor rather than retaliating against him. This is precisely the "slave philosophy" the Muslims have sought to escape in their repudiation of Christianity. Hence, King represents to the Muslims a capitulation to the cunning Christian strategy of the white man.[29]

On a television interview in June 1963, when asked if Martin Luther King's movement and demonstrations had been successful in Birmingham, Malcolm X responded with:

No, No. What kind of success did they get in Birmingham? A chance to sit at a lunch counter and drink some coffee with a cracker—that's success? A chance to—thousands of little children went to jail; they didn't get out, they were bonded out by King. They had to *pay* their way out of jail. That's not any kind of advancement or success.[30]

Malcolm's attitudes toward civil-rights leaders, his advocacy of the separation of the races, and some of his other views presented in the Cornell University debate underwent a change in 1964, a year before his assassination. After his 1964 pilgrimage to Mecca, Malcolm X said:

In the past, yes, I have made sweeping indictments of all white people. I never will be guilty of that again—as I know now that some white people are truly sincere, that some truly are capable of being brotherly toward a black man. The true Islam has shown me that a blanket indictment of all white people is as wrong as when whites make blanket indictments against blacks.[31]

As for civil-rights leaders of CORE, SNCC, NAACP, and SCLC, he said a year before his death:

I am prepared to cooperate in local civil-rights actions in the South and elsewhere and shall do so because every campaign for specific objectives can only heighten the political consciousness of the Negroes and intensify their identification against white society. . . . There is no use deceiving ourselves. Good education, housing and jobs are imperatives for the Negroes, and I shall support them in their fight to win these objectives, but I shall tell Negroes that while these are necessary, they cannot solve the main Negro problem.[32]

In 1962, however, Malcolm X was attempting to persuade audiences that integration was not the answer to America's racial conflict, that Negroes and whites should reject the hypocrisy of the token integration that was taking place, that Negroes should work toward separate societies for blacks and whites, that if whites wanted to help resolve the conflicts between blacks and whites they should work among other whites and not among Negroes. By 1967, several civil-rights leaders and organizations had come to accept some of Malcolm's ideas. What seemed objectionable in 1962 eventually came to appear less objectionable in 1967.

Malcolm's opponent in the Cornell University debate of March 7, 1962, was James Farmer who organized the interracial Congress of Racial Equality in 1942. Unlike the Black Muslim organizations, CORE has always been interracial and, in 1961, when the freedom rides to Alabama and Mississippi were taking place, two thirds of its membership and staff were whites. CORE became active, especially in the 1950s and 1960s, in desegregating buses, lunch counters, swimming pools, bus terminals; its members conducted "shop-ins" to persuade store owners to halt job discrimination and picketed to protest segregated housing. CORE's most publicized civil-rights protest activities were the freedom rides of 1961, interracial demonstrations attempting to desegregate facilities in interstate travel. As Lerone Bennett, Jr., observed, CORE brought to the civil-rights movement a history of "non-violent direct action and a tough, to-the-wall posture." [33] Those Negroes who felt that the presence of white people in "Negro" civil-rights organizations inevitably led to "go-slowism" had to recognize that CORE was one of the more militant civil-rights action groups. Louis Lomax has written of the nature and spirit of CORE:

The genius of CORE . . . is its insistence that direct mass action is the only way for Negroes to realize the practical results of the towering legal decisions the NAACP has won. CORE's argument for mass action embraces a good deal more than gathering people together for a demonstration; it goes to the root of having the job done by the people rather than for them; it underscores the fact that better response is gotten from the masses when the issue involved is a service open to great numbers of people rather than to a few. . . . CORE moves in peace but, to a man, its demonstrators are ready to endure the hardships of war. And this, in essence, is the underlying spirit of the Negro revolt.[34]

By 1967, the role of whites in CORE, then under the leadership of Floyd McKissick, was reduced and CORE turned to black power; a one-time CORE public relations man pointed out that the de-emphasis of the role of whites in CORE was inevitable and consistent: "Essentially the whole interracial thrust of the civil-rights movement has been significant, but tragically weak. Nothing substantial was accomplished. You can walk into an American ghetto today and see no substantial difference since 1960." [35]

The role of whites in the civil-rights movement became more and more of a controversy within the movement itself. This controversy was especially prominent during the civil-rights march, jointly sponsored by CORE, SNCC, and SCLC, which carried on James Meredith's freedom march through Mississippi after Meredith had been shot from ambush along his march route in June 1966. During this second phase of the march, the question of the participation of whites was raised. Martin Luther King told those persons who wanted to turn the march into a "Negro" march that "I could not in good conscience agree to continue my personal involvement and that of SCLC in the march if it were not publicly affirmed that it was based on nonviolence and the participation of both black and white." After some discussion, Stokely Carmichael of SNCC and Floyd McKissick of CORE agreed that they "could unite around these principles as far as the march was concerned." [36] Several days later, the marchers reached Greenwood, Mississippi, and Martin Luther King recorded the events and conversations that took place at this stage of the march and the "birth of the Black Power slogan in the civil-rights movement." King's observations merit extended quotation here, for what he has recorded deals directly with one aspect of the rhetoric of the civil-rights movement, that is, the use of language and the effect of slogans. King wrote in *Where Do We Go from Here: Chaos or Community?*:

As the days progressed, debates and discussions continued, but they were usually pushed to the background by the onrush of enthusiasm engendered by the large crowds that turned out to greet us in every town. We had been marching for about ten days when we passed through Grenada on the way to Greenwood. Stokely did not conceal his growing eagerness to reach Greenwood. This was SNCC territory, in the sense that the organization had worked courageously there during that turbulent summer of 1964.

As we approached the city, large crowds of old friends and new turned out to welcome us. At a huge mass meeting that night, which was held in a city park, Stokely mounted the platform and after arousing the audience with a powerful attack on Mississippi justice, he proclaimed: "What we need is black power." Willie Ricks, the fiery orator of SNCC, leaped to the platform and shouted, "What do you want?" The crowd roared, "Black Power." Again and again Ricks cried, "What do you want?" and the response "Black Power" grew louder and louder, until it had reached fever pitch.

So Greenwood turned out to be the arena for the birth of the Black Power slogan in the civil rights movement. The phrase had been used long before by Richard Wright and others, but never until that night had it been used as a slogan in the civil rights movement. For people who had been crushed so long by white power and who had been taught that black was degrading, it had a ready appeal.

Immediately, however, I had reservations about its use. I had the deep feeling that it was an unfortunate choice of words for a slogan. Moreover, I saw it bringing about division within the ranks of the marchers. For a day or two there was fierce competition between those who were wedded to the Black Power slogan and those wedded to Freedom Now. Speakers on each side sought desperately to get the crowds to chant their slogan the loudest.

Sensing this widening split in our ranks, I asked Stokely and Floyd to join me in a frank discussion of the problem. We met the next morning, along with members of each of our staffs, in a small Catholic parish house in Yazoo City. For five long hours I pleaded with the group to abandon the Black Power slogan. It was my contention that a leader has to be concerned about the problem of semantics. Each word, I said, has a denotative meaning—its explicit and recognized sense—and a connotative meaning—its suggestive sense. While the concept of legitimate Black Power might be denotatively sound, the slogan "Black Power" carried the wrong connotations. I mentioned the implications of violence that the press had already attached to the phrase. And I went on to say that some of the rash statements on the part of a few marchers only reinforced this impression.

Stokely replied by saying that the question of violence versus nonviolence was irrelevant. The real question was the need for black people to consolidate their political and economic resources to achieve power. "Power," he said, "is the only thing respected in this world, and we must get it at any cost." Then he looked me squarely in the eye and said, "Martin, you know as well as I do that practically every other ethnic group in America has done just this. The Jews, the Irish and the Italians did it, why can't we?"

"That is just the point," I answered. "No one has ever heard the Jews publicly chant a slogan of Jewish power, but they have power. Through group unity, determination and creative endeavor, they have gained it. The same thing is true of the Irish and Italians. Neither group has used a slogan of Irish or Italian power, but they have worked hard to achieve it. This is exactly what we must do," I said. "We must use every constructive means to amass economic and political power. This is the kind of legitimate power we need. We must work to build racial pride and refute the notion that black is evil and ugly. But this must come through a program, not merely through a slogan."

Stokely and Floyd insisted that the slogan itself was important. "How can you arouse people to unite around a program without a slogan as a rallying cry? Didn't the labor movement have slogans? Haven't we had slogans all along in the freedom movement? What we need is a new slogan with 'black' in it."

I conceded the fact that we must have slogans. But why have

one that would confuse our allies, isolate the Negro community and give many prejudiced whites, who might otherwise be ashamed of their anti-Negro feeling, a ready excuse for self-justification?

"Why not use the slogan 'black consciousness' or 'black equality'?" I suggested. "These phrases would be less vulnerable and would more accurately describe what we are about. The words 'black' and 'power' together give the impression that we are talking about black domination rather than black equality."

Stokely responded that neither would have the ready appeal and persuasive force of Black Power. Throughout the lengthy discussion, Stokely and Floyd remained adamant, and Stokely concluded by saying, with candor, "Martin, I deliberately decided to raise this issue on the march in order to give it a national forum, and force you to take a stand for Black Power."

I laughed. "I have been used before," I said to Stokely. "One more time won't hurt."

The meeting ended with the SCLC staff members still agreeing with me that the slogan was unfortunate and would only divert attention from the evils of Mississippi, while most CORE and SNCC staff members joined Stokely and Floyd in insisting that it should be projected nationally. In a final attempt to maintain unity I suggested that we compromise by not chanting either "Black Power" or "Freedom Now" for the rest of the march. In this way neither the people nor the press would be confused by the apparent conflict, and staff members would not appear to be at loggerheads. They all agreed with this compromise.

But while the chant died out, the press kept the debate going. News stories now centered, not on the injustices of Mississippi, but on the apparent ideological division in the civil rights movement. Every revolutionary movement has its peaks of united activity and its valleys of debate and internal confusion. This debate might well have been little more than a healthy internal difference of opinion, but the press loves the sensational and it could not allow the issue to remain within the private domain of the movement. In every drama there has to be an antagonist and a protagonist, and if the antagonist is not there the press will find and build one.[37]

Carmichael was not the first to express the idea of black power. As King points out, the phrase had been used earlier by Richard Wright and others. In his book *The Fire Next Time*, published in 1963, James Baldwin, after discussing that there was very little in the white man's value system for the Negroes to emulate, wrote: "The only thing white people have that black people need, or should want, is power—and no one holds power forever." [38] The key to the Negro's struggle, said Lerone Bennett, Jr., in 1965, "is not race but conflict, not words but power. In the black beginning . . . was not a word but a fact: white power." [39] Speaking to the graduating class at Howard University on May 26, 1966, Adam Clayton Powell asserted:

Civil rights has been that grand deception practiced by those who have not placed God first, who have not believed that God-given rights can empower the black man with superiority as well as equality. . . . To demand these God-given human rights is to seek black power, what I call audacious power—the power to build black institutions of splendid achievement. . . . [40]

After Carmichael's use of black power was publicized, the immediate response among most whites was fear and anxiety; as one civil-rights worker put it, the response was "white fright." The reaction of the whites bore out King's contention, in his discussion with Carmichael and McKissick, that "the words 'black' and 'power' together give the impression that we [Negroes] are talking about black domination rather than black equality." Carmichael himself recognized the whites' fearful and anxious response to the slogan of black power, but to him this only demonstrated that he had hit upon a slogan with great impact. Speaking to a predominantly Negro audience in Seattle in 1967, Carmichael said: "You ought to know that anything they [whites] are against you should automatically be for. That's how come we knew Black Power was so good. We said the word and the whole white world came out against it. We said, 'That's it. We got it. Black Power. We got it.' "

During 1966 and 1967, while the black-power spokesmen were making it clear that there was less and less of a place for white people in their organizations, less militant civil-rights leaders saw black power as a kind of "black racism." Martin Luther King, admitting that the Negro needed to develop a sense of dignity and pride and also that the Negro needed to attain

"power," explained: "My problem with sncc is not their militancy. I think you can be militantly nonviolent. It's what I see
as a pattern of violence emerging and their use of the cry,
'black power,' which, whether they mean it or not, falls on the
ear as racism in reverse." [41] Roy Wilkins, executive director of
the naacp, observed nothing positive in black power; Wilkins
devoted a significant part of his keynote address (included here,
pp. 89–100), delivered in Los Angeles on July 5, 1966, at the
naacp's Fifty-seventh Annual Convention, to a condemnation
of black power. While Wilkins devoted the major portion of
his speech to the goals and tactics of the naacp which, among
the various civil-rights organizations, has primarily emphasized
achieving equality, justice, and integration for the Negro
through the courts and through legislation, and less through
persuasion by the use of demonstrations, sit-ins, and freedom
rides, he made clear to his audience of about a thousand dele-
gates that the naacp disassociated itself from black power.[42]

One effect of the slogan was the alienation of many whites
who were one-time supporters of sncc's programs; sncc experienced a loss in some needed financial support. John Lewis,
Carmichael's predecessor as sncc's national chairman, predicted
just such a reaction. In July 1966, Lewis charged that sncc's
"new rhetoric—no matter what its intent—risked alienating
white allies." [43] In an effort to regain some of this support, sncc
mailed a short letter from Carmichael to potential supporters
urging the recipient to "stick with us"; a pamphlet that accom-
panied the letter explained what Carmichael meant by black
power. That pamphlet, included in this book (pp. 101–108), was
a shortened version of an article Carmichael had written for
The New York Review of Books, which has predominantly
"white liberal" subscribers, the whites who apparently needed
to be persuaded to continue their support of sncc.

In 1967, Carmichael toured United States campuses and, as
Newsweek charged, he was "soaking whites $1,000 for a rather
tame exposition of black power, charging Negro colleges $500
for the gloves-off treatment." [44] Although the pamphlet included here is not a speech, it is an example of Carmichael's

ability to adapt his material to his audience; the pamphlet is a "rather tame exposition" of what he meant by black power. His Morgan State College Speech of January 16, 1967 (see pp. 109–125), presented to Negro college students, exemplifies Carmichael's "gloves-off treatment." The difference in style is directly related to Carmichael's rhetorical purposes; he is asking something different from each audience, and hence each audience requires a different style. However, in both the pamphlet and the Morgan State College Speech, Carmichael deals essentially with similar material: identity, definition of self, exploitation, property, and violence. In neither case is his the rhetoric of the more moderate civil-rights leaders. In some comments about the language of "love and suffering," "the American dream," "non-violence," and "integration," Carmichael has said:

The advocates of Black Power reject the old slogans and meaningless rhetoric of previous years in the civil rights struggle. The language of yesterday is indeed irrelevant: progress, non-violence, integration, fear of "white backlash," coalition. Let us look at the rhetoric and see why these terms must be set aside.[45]

Another black-power advocate, Floyd McKissick, who in 1966 replaced James Farmer as national director of CORE, outlined that organization's philosophy of black power; he stated in 1966 that

black people must decide for themselves. They must have self-determination to determine the direction and the pace in which they will become total citizens in this society. And in doing so, six basic ingredients are needed: One, political power. Two, economic power. Three, an improved self-image of the black man himself—as you well know that is not in the history books, what we have done and the contributions we have made. Four, the development of young militant leadership. Five, the enforcement of Federal laws, abolishment of police brutality. And six, the development of a black consumer bloc.[46]

One year later, McKissick delivered a speech to a group of about seven hundred Negroes from all over the United States who met in Newark, New Jersey, for a black-power conference.

This speech of July 21, 1967 (included here, pp. 127–142) revealed an increased militancy in CORE leadership; late in the speech McKissick talks of revolution, asserting that "even white men recognized the need for revolution when, in 1776, they revolted because they were oppressed. And today—1967—black people are more oppressed than any white man has ever been in the history of the world." This militancy in McKissick's speech may partly be explained by the fact that it was delivered to a group of Negro leaders who saw in black power some hope of doing away with the injustices, indignities, and violence against the Negroes of America. As *The New York Times* explained:

For one thing, the size and diversity of the conference made it clear that the "Black Power" slogan contains a kind of magnetism that cannot be totally ignored by those Negroes who hope for influence in the nation's ghettos. While Black Power leaders still have to prove they can work together, they are beginning to demonstrate they can work against anyone who scoffs at the Black Power phrase.[47]

In his speech, McKissick does not speak of the "Negro"; instead, he speaks of the "black man." He does not speak of the "civil-rights movement"; CORE, McKissick said, is no longer a civil-rights organization: "Forget about civil rights. I'm talking about black power." [48]

In his speech to the black-power conference, McKissick, after developing the idea that white Americans are not above practicing genocide against the blacks in the United States, declares: "This is not a problem of civil rights. It is a problem of black survival. The concept of civil rights is pitifully insignificant when our very lives are at stake." McKissick, as well as other so-called radical civil-rights leaders, defines individual followers as "black men" who achieve "black power" through group action. "Black men" and "black power" emphasize racial differences obscured by the slogans of the integrationists. This emphasis on blackness can be seen as one means in a desperate search for self-definition, a selfhood, an identity so long denied to the Negro by the white majority. Though the psychological soundness of self-definition based on color may well be argued, it is the pride of being black that is the positive aspect of the black-power movement. In its negative manifestation, the ideas and utterances of black-power leaders reveal the final consequence of the separation of men into black and white, inferior and superior, oppressed and oppressor—namely, such a total lack of communication that the dominant power group does not even consider those it oppresses human. The specter of genocide begins to haunt the imagination and experience of the oppressed. Thus McKissick argues that any group which demands of the white exploiters "Take your foot off our back" will be exterminated. McKissick asks and answers: "Would America exterminate twenty-two million blacks? . . . Look at the record! More specifically, I believe they can. I believe they will." With such a view of total oppression, the Negro has little to gain and nothing to lose. Black power becomes a means of gaining dignity.

In spite of its fierceness, however, McKissick's speech communicates a feeling of desperation that contrasts strongly with the hope and trust of the integrationists who envisioned "black and white together." Though black-power spokesmen heighten separatism and the lack of communication between blacks and whites, they are not to blame. For the cause of separatism is to be sought among the whites who have claimed to "understand our darkies," who have written "mammy" on the tombstone of their children's nurse without even dignifying the woman with her first name or her last name, which belonged not to her family but to her master. The cause is to be sought in the endless line of typical Negro maids and houseboys who shuffled, giggled, and shrieked in American films and plays. In their stylized roles they were dehumanized and yet thought to be typically Negro by the white majority. The cause is to be sought in the white man's language about the blacks, a language which concocts such things as "the Negro problem." In a discussion of the reasons why racism continues to exist in America, Lerone Bennett, Jr., writes:

We do not come up with the right answers to our problems because we seldom ask ourselves the right question. There is no Negro problem in America; there has never been a Negro problem in America —the problem of race in America is a white problem. To understand that problem and to control it, we must address ourselves to the fears and frailties of white people.[49]

The cause is to be sought in white America's definition of "who is a Negro"; legalisms have defined America into the blacks and the whites.

Whatever else black-power spokesmen have accomplished, they have focused the attention of black and white Americans on the fact that the blacks of America have allowed themselves to be defined by the white people. The civil-rights movement in its various manifestations tries to give the Negro a role that is self-chosen and not impressed on him from without. The disagreement among the various civil-rights groups can be seen in light of the attempts to discover identity. What is that identity? Is the Negro to emulate the white man? Is the Negro "like" the white man? Is he quite different, designed to inconvenience the white? The black-power movement wants to be an inconvenience and, as such, presents a change from one rhetorical strategy to another. The success or failure, the consequence of such rhetorical choices, remains to be seen.

NOTES

1. Martin Luther King, Jr., *Stride Toward Freedom* (New York: Harper & Row, 1958), p. 70.

2. Louis E. Lomax, *The Negro Revolt* (New York: Harper & Bros., 1962), p. 81.

3. Lerone Bennett, Jr., *Confrontation: Black and White* (Chicago: Johnson, 1965), p. 227.

4. Roland T. Heacock, *Understanding the Negro Protest* (New York: Pageant, 1965), p. 8.

5. Arthur Waskow, *From Race Riot to Sit-in* (Garden City, N. Y.: Doubleday, 1966), p. 227.

6. James H. Laue, "The Changing Character of Negro Protest," *The Annals*, January 1965, p. 121.

7. King, *op. cit.*, pp. 215–216.

8. Roy Wilkins, "What Now? One Negro Leader's Answer," *The New York Times Magazine*, August 16, 1964, p. 11, p. 15.

9. *Garner v. Louisiana*, 368 U.S. 157 (1961).

10. Harry Kalven, Jr., *The Negro and the First Amendment* (Columbus, Ohio: Ohio State University Press, 1965), p. 133.

11. Milton R. Konvitz, *Expanding Liberties* (New York: Viking, 1966), p. 315.

12. Donald Matthews and James Prothro, *Negroes and the New Southern Politics* (New York: Harcourt, Brace & World, 1966), p. 434.

13. Franklyn Haiman, "The Rhetoric of the Streets: Some Legal and Ethical Considerations," *Quarterly Journal of Speech*, April 1967, p. 49.

14. Leonard Doob, *Propaganda: Its Psychology and Technique* (New York: Holt, 1935), p. 402.

15. Waskow, *op. cit.*, p. 232.

16. Lerone Bennett, Jr., *What Manner of Man* (New York: Simon & Schuster, 1965), p. 114.

17. Martin Luther King, Jr., *Where Do We Go from Here: Chaos or Community?* (New York: Harper & Row, 1967), pp. 17–18.

18. Waskow, *op. cit.*, p. 234.

19. Martin Luther King, Jr., *Why We Can't Wait* (New York: Harper & Row, 1964), p. 78.

20. Kenneth B. Clark, *Dark Ghetto* (New York: Harper & Row, 1965), p. 202.

21. *Ibid.*

22. Bennett, *Confrontation: Black and White*, *op. cit.*, p. 285.

23. Murray Kempton, "The March on Washington," *The New Republic*, September 14, 1963, pp. 19–20.

24. Malcolm Little, *Autobiography of Malcolm X* (New York: Grove, 1965), p. 284.

25. C. Eric Lincoln, *The Black Muslims in America* (Boston: Beacon, 1961), pp. 18–19.

26. Little, *op. cit.*, pp. 379–380.

27. Simeon Booker, *Black Man's America* (Englewood Cliffs, N.J.: Prentice-Hall, 1964), p. 126.

28. Lincoln, *op. cit.*, p. 148.

29. *Ibid.*, p. 152.

30. Kenneth B. Clark, *The Negro Protest* (Boston: Beacon, 1963), p. 27.

31. Little, *op. cit.*, p. 382.

32. Malcolm Little, *Malcolm X Speaks* (New York: Grove, 1965), p. 18.

33. Bennett, *Confrontation: Black and White, op. cit.*, p. 269.

34. Lomax, *op. cit.*, p. 146.

35. *The New York Times Magazine*, October 1, 1967, p. 99.

36. King, *Where Do We Go from Here: Chaos or Community?, op. cit.*, pp. 28–29.

37. *Ibid.*, pp. 29–32.

38. James Baldwin, *The Fire Next Time* (New York: Dial, 1963), p. 110.

39. Bennett, *Confrontation: Black and White, op. cit.*, p. 10.

40. *U.S. News and World Report*, June 13, 1966, p. 14.

41. Fred Powledge, *Black Power—White Resistance* (Cleveland: World, 1967), p. 238.

42. See *The New York Times*, July 6–10, 1966, for coverage of this convention.

43. *Newsweek*, July 11, 1966, p. 32.

44. *Newsweek*, May 15, 1967, p. 28.

45. Stokely Carmichael and Charles V. Hamilton, *Black Power: The Politics of Liberation in America* (New York: Random House, 1967), p. 50.

46. Powledge, *op. cit.*, p. 239.

47. *The New York Times*, July 23, 1967.

48. *The New York Times Magazine*, October 1, 1967, pp. 32–33.

49. Bennett, *Confrontation: Black and White, op. cit.*, p. 298.

Public Statement by
Eight Alabama Clergymen

APRIL 12, 1963

We the undersigned clergymen are among those who, in January, issued "An Appeal for Law and Order and Common Sense," in dealing with racial problems in Alabama. We expressed understanding that honest convictions in racial matters could properly be pursued in the courts, but urged that decisions of those courts should in the meantime be peacefully obeyed.

Since that time there had been some evidence of increased forbearance and a willingness to face facts. Responsible citizens have undertaken to work on various problems which cause racial friction and unrest. In Birmingham, recent public events have given indication that we all have opportunity for a new constructive and realistic approach to racial problems.

However, we are now confronted by a series of demonstrations by some of our Negro citizens, directed and led in part by outsiders. We recognize the natural impatience of people who feel that their hopes are slow in being realized. But we are convinced that these demonstrations are unwise and untimely.

We agree rather with certain local Negro leadership which has called for honest and open negotiation of racial issues in our area. And we believe this kind of facing of issues can best be accomplished by citizens of our own metropolitan area, white and Negro, meeting with their knowledge and experience of the local situation. All of us need to face that responsibility and find proper channels for its accomplishment.

Just as we formerly pointed out that "hatred and violence have no sanction in our religious and political traditions," we also point out that such actions as incite to hatred and violence, however technically peaceful those actions may be, have not contributed to the resolution of our local problems. We do not believe that these days of new hope are days when extreme measures are justified in Birmingham.

We commend the community as a whole, and the local news media and law enforcement officials in particular, on the calm manner in which these demonstrations have been handled. We urge the public to continue to show restraint should the demonstrations continue, and the law enforcement officials to remain calm and continue to protect our city from violence.

We further strongly urge our own Negro community to withdraw support from these demonstrations, and to unite locally in working peacefully for a better Birmingham. When rights are consistently denied, a cause should be pressed in the courts and in negotiations among local leaders, and not in the streets. We appeal to both our white and Negro citizenry to observe the principles of law and order and common sense.

Signed by:

C. C. J. CARPENTER, D.D., LL.D., Bishop of Alabama

JOSEPH A. DURICK, D.D., Auxiliary Bishop, Diocese of Mobile–Birmingham

RABBI MILTON L. GRAFMAN, Temple Emanu-El, Birmingham, Alabama

BISHOP PAUL HARDIN, Bishop of the Alabama–West Florida Conference of the Methodist Church

BISHOP NOLAN B. HARMON, Bishop of the North Alabama Conference of the Methodist Church

GEORGE M. MURRAY, D.D., LL.D., Bishop Coadjutor, Episcopal Diocese of Alabama

EDWARD V. RAMAGE, Moderator, Synod of the Alabama Presbyterian Church in the United States

EARL STALLINGS, Pastor, First Baptist Church, Birmingham, Alabama

MARTIN LUTHER KING, JR.

Letter from Birmingham City Jail

APRIL 16, 1963

Martin Luther King, Jr., was born in Atlanta, Georgia, on January 15, 1929. He graduated from Morehouse College with a B.A. degree in 1948; in 1955, he received his Ph.D. degree from Boston University. In 1957, he was elected president of the Southern Christian Leadership Conference (SCLC). In 1964, Martin Luther King, Jr., won the Nobel Peace Prize, the youngest man ever to be awarded that prize. He was assassinated in Memphis, Tennessee, on April 4, 1968.

MY DEAR FELLOW CLERGYMEN,

While confined here in the Birmingham City Jail, I came across your recent statement calling our present activities "unwise and untimely." Seldom, if ever, do I pause to answer criticism of my work and ideas. If I sought to answer all of the criticisms that cross my desk, my secretaries would be engaged in little else in the course of the day and I would have no time for constructive work. But since I feel that you are men of genuine good will and your criticisms are sincerely set forth, I would like to answer your statement in what I hope will be patient and reasonable terms.

I think I should give the reason for my being in Birmingham, since you have been influenced by the argument of "outsiders coming in." I have the honor of serving as president of the Southern Christian Leadership Conference, an organization operating in every Southern state with headquarters in Atlanta, Georgia. We have some eighty-five affiliate organizations all across the South—one being the Alabama Christian Movement for Human Rights. Whenever necessary and possible we share staff, educational, and financial resources with our affiliates. Several months ago our local affiliate here in Birmingham invited us to be on call to engage in a nonviolent direct action program if such were deemed necessary. We readily consented and when the hour came we lived up to our promises. So I am here, along with several members of my staff, because we were invited here. I am here because I have basic organizational ties here. Beyond this, I am in Birmingham because injustice is here. Just as the eighth-century prophets left their little villages and carried their "thus saith the Lord" far beyond the boundaries of their home town, and just as the Apostle Paul left his little village of Tarsus and carried the gospel of Jesus Christ to practically every hamlet and city of the Graeco-Roman world, I too am compelled to carry the gospel of freedom beyond my particular home town. Like Paul, I must constantly respond to the Macedonian call for aid.[1]

Moreover, I am cognizant of the interrelatedness of all communities and states. I cannot sit idly by in Atlanta and not be concerned about what happens in Birmingham. Injustice anywhere is a threat to justice everywhere. We are caught in an inescapable network of mutuality tied in a single garment of destiny. Whatever affects one directly affects all indirectly. Never again can we afford to live with the narrow, provincial "outside agitator" idea. Anyone who lives inside the United States can never be considered an outsider anywhere in this country.

You deplore the demonstrations that are presently taking place in Birmingham. But I am sorry that your statement did not express a similar concern for the conditions that brought the demonstrations into being. I am sure that each of you would want to go beyond the superficial social analyst who looks

[1] What possible rhetorical effects could this analogy have upon King's audience?

merely at effects, and does not grapple with underlying causes. I would not hesitate to say that it is unfortunate that so-called demonstrations are taking place in Birmingham at this time, but I would say in more emphatic terms that it is even more unfortunate that the white power structure of this city left the Negro community with no other alternative.

In any nonviolent campaign there are four basic steps: (1) collection of the facts to determine whether injustices are alive; (2) negotiation; (3) self-purification; and (4) direct action. We have gone through all of these steps in Birmingham. There can be no gainsaying of the fact that racial injustice engulfs this community. Birmingham is probably the most thoroughly segregated city in the United States. Its ugly record of police brutality is known in every section of this country. Its unjust treatment of Negroes in the courts is a notorious reality. There have been more unsolved bombings of Negro homes and churches in Birmingham than any city in this nation. These are the hard, brutal, and unbelievable facts. On the basis of these conditions Negro leaders sought to negotiate with the city fathers. But the political leaders consistently refused to engage in good faith negotiation.

Then came the opportunity last September to talk with some of the leaders of the economic community. In these negotiating sessions certain promises were made by the merchants—such as the promise to remove the humiliating racial signs from the stores. On the basis of these promises Reverend Shuttlesworth and the leaders of the Alabama Christian Movement for Human Rights agreed to call a moratorium on any type of demonstrations. As the weeks and months unfolded we realized that we were the victims of a broken promise. The signs remained. As in so many experiences of the past, we were confronted with blasted hopes, and the dark shadow of a deep disappointment settled upon us. So we had no alternative except that of preparing for direct action, whereby we would present our very bodies as a means of laying our case before the conscience of the local and national community. We were not unmindful of the difficulties involved. So we decided to go through a process of self-purification. We started having workshops on nonviolence and repeatedly asked ourselves the questions, "Are you able to accept blows without retaliating?" "Are you able to endure the ordeals of jail?"

We decided to set our direct action program around the Easter season, realizing that, with the exception of Christmas, this was the largest shopping period of the year. Knowing that a strong economic withdrawal program would be the by-product of direct action, we felt that this was the best time to bring pressure on the merchants for the needed changes. Then it occurred to us that the March election was ahead, and so we speedily decided to postpone action until after election day. When we discovered that Mr. [Eugene "Bull"] Connor was in the run-off, we decided again to postpone action so that the demonstrations could not be used to cloud the issues. At this time we agreed to begin our nonviolent witness the day after the run-off.

This reveals that we did not move irresponsibly into direct action. We too wanted to see Mr. Connor defeated; so we went through postponement after postponement to aid in this community need. After this we felt that direct action could be delayed no longer.

You may well ask, "Why direct action? Why sit-ins, marches, etc.? Isn't negotiation a better path?" You are exactly right in your call for negotiation. Indeed, this is the purpose of direct action. Nonviolent direct action seeks to create such a crisis and establish such creative tension that a community that has constantly refused to negotiate is forced to confront the issue. It seeks so to dramatize the issue that it can no longer be ignored.

I just referred to the creation of tension as a part of the work of the nonviolent resister. This may sound rather shocking. But I must confess that I am not afraid of the word tension. I have earnestly worked and preached against violent tension, but there is a type of constructive nonviolent tension that is necessary for growth. Just as Socrates felt that it was necessary to create a tension in the mind so that individuals could rise from the bondage of myths and half-truths to the unfettered realm of creative analysis and objective appraisal, we must see the need of having nonviolent gadflies to create the kind of tension in society that will help men rise from the dark depths of prejudice and racism to the majestic heights of understanding and brotherhood. So the purpose of the direct action is to create a situation so crisis-packed that it will inevitably open the door to negotiation. We, therefore, concur with you in your call for negotiation. Too long has our beloved Southland been bogged down in the tragic attempt to live in monologue rather than dialogue.

One of the basic points in your statement is that our acts are untimely. Some have asked, "Why didn't you give the new administration time to act?" The only answer that I can give to this inquiry is that the new administration must be prodded about as much as the outgoing one before it acts. We will be sadly mistaken if we feel that the election of Mr. [Albert] Boutwell will bring the millennium to Birmingham. While Mr. Boutwell is much more articulate and gentle than Mr. Connor, they are both segregationists dedicated to the task of maintaining the status quo. The hope I see in Mr. Boutwell is that he will be reasonable enough to see the futility of massive resistance to desegregation. But he will not see this without pressure from the devotees of civil rights.

My friends, I must say to you that we have not made a single gain in civil rights without determined legal and nonviolent pressure. History is the long and tragic story of the fact that privileged groups seldom give up their privileges voluntarily. Individuals may see the moral light and voluntarily give up their unjust posture; but as Reinhold Niebuhr has reminded us, groups are more immoral than individuals.

We know through painful experience that freedom is never voluntarily given by the oppressor; it must be demanded by the oppressed. Frankly I have never yet engaged in a direct action movement that was "well timed," according to the timetable of those who have not suffered unduly from the disease of segregation. For years now I have heard the word "Wait!" It rings in the ear of every Negro with a piercing familiarity. This "wait" has almost always meant "never." It has been a tranquilizing Thalidomide, relieving the emotional stress for a moment, only to give birth to an ill-formed infant of frustration. We must come to see with the distinguished jurist of yesterday that "justice too long delayed is justice denied." We have waited for more than 340 years for our constitutional and God-given rights. The nations of Asia and Africa are moving with jet-like speed toward the goal of political independence, and we still creep at horse and buggy pace toward the gaining of a cup of coffee at a lunch counter.

I guess it is easy for those who have never felt the stinging darts of segregation to say wait. But when you have seen vicious mobs lynch your mothers and fathers at will and drown your sisters and brothers at whim; when you have seen hate-filled policemen curse, kick, brutalize, and even kill your black brothers and sisters with impunity; when you see the vast majority of your twenty million Negro brothers smothering in an air-tight cage of poverty in the midst of an affluent society; when you suddenly find your tongue twisted and your speech stammering as you seek to explain to your six-year-old daughter why she can't go to the public amusement park that has just been advertised on television, and see tears welling up in her little eyes when she is told that Funtown is closed to colored children, and see the depressing clouds of inferiority begin to form in her little mental sky, and see her begin to distort her little personality by unconsciously developing a bitterness toward white people; when you have to concoct an answer for a five-year-old son asking in agonizing pathos: "Daddy, why do white people treat colored people so mean?"; when you take a cross country drive and find it necessary to sleep night after night in the uncomfortable corners of your automobile because no motel will accept you; when you are humiliated day in and day out by nagging signs reading "white" men and "colored"; when your first name becomes "nigger" and your middle name becomes "boy" (however old you are) and your last name becomes "John," and when your wife and mother are never given the respected title "Mrs."; when you are harried by day and haunted by night by the fact that you are a Negro, living constantly at tip-toe stance never quite knowing what to expect next, and plagued with inner fears and outer resentments; when you are forever fighting a degenerating sense of "nobodiness"—then you will understand why we find it difficult to wait.[2] There comes a time when the cup of endurance runs over, and men are no longer willing to be plunged into an abyss of injustice where they experience the bleakness of corroding despair. I hope, sirs, you can understand our legitimate and unavoidable impatience.

You express a great deal of anxiety over our willingness to break laws. This is certainly a legitimate concern. Since we so diligently urge people to obey the Supreme Court's decision of 1954 outlawing segregation in the public schools, it is rather strange and paradoxical to find us consciously breaking laws. One may well ask, "How can you advocate breaking some laws and obeying others?" The answer is found in the fact that there are two types of laws: There are *just* laws and there are *unjust* laws. I would be the first to advocate obeying just laws. One has not only a legal but a moral responsibility to obey just laws. Conversely, one has a moral responsibility to disobey unjust laws. I would agree with Saint Augustine that "An unjust law is no law at all."

Now what is the difference between the two? How does one determine when a law is just or unjust? A just law is a man-made code that squares with the moral law or the law of God. An unjust law is a mode that is out of harmony with the moral law. To put it in the terms of Saint Thomas Aquinas, an unjust law is a human law that is not rooted in eternal and natural law. Any law that uplifts human personality is just. Any law that degrades human personality is unjust.

All segregation statutes are unjust because segregation distorts the soul and damages the personality. It gives the segregator a false sense of superiority and the segregated a false sense of inferiority. To use the words of Martin Buber, the great Jewish philosopher, segregation substitutes an "I-it" relationship for the "I-thou" relationship, and ends up relegating persons to the

[2] What is the rhetorical effect of this long, periodic sentence?

status of things. So segregation is not only politically, economically, and sociologically unsound, but it is morally wrong and sinful. Paul Tillich has said that sin is separation. Isn't segregation an existential expression of man's tragic separation, an expression of his awful estrangement, his terrible sinfulness? So I can urge men to obey the 1954 decision of the Supreme Court because it is morally right, and I can urge them to disobey segregation ordinances because they are morally wrong.[3]

Let us turn to a more concrete example of just and unjust laws. An unjust law is a code that a majority inflicts on a minority that is not binding on itself. This is *difference* made legal. On the other hand a just law is a code that a majority compels a minority to follow that it is willing to follow itself. This is *sameness* made legal.

Let me give another explanation. An unjust law is a code inflicted upon a minority which that minority had no part in enacting or creating because they did not have the unhampered right to vote. Who can say the legislature of Alabama which set up the segregation laws was democratically elected? Throughout the state of Alabama all types of conniving methods are used to prevent Negroes from becoming registered voters and there are some counties without a single Negro registered to vote despite the fact that the Negro constitutes a majority of the population. Can any law set up in such a state be considered democratically structured?

These are just a few examples of unjust and just laws. There are some instances when a law is just on its face but unjust in its application. For instance, I was arrested Friday on a charge of parading without a permit. Now there is nothing wrong with an ordinance which requires a permit for a parade, but when the ordinance is used to preserve segregation and to deny citizens the First Amendment privilege of peaceful assembly and peaceful protest, then it becomes unjust.

I hope you can see the distinction I am trying to point out. In no sense do I advocate evading or defying the law as the rabid

[3] What are the two deductive arguments presented in this paragraph? Are they valid arguments?

segregationist would do. This would lead to anarchy. One who breaks an unjust law must do it *openly, lovingly* (not hatefully as the white mothers did in New Orleans when they were seen on television screaming "nigger, nigger, nigger") and with a willingness to accept the penalty. I submit that an individual who breaks a law that conscience tells him is unjust, and willingly accepts the penalty by staying in jail to arouse the conscience of the community over its injustice, is in reality expressing the very highest respect for law.[4]

Of course there is nothing new about this kind of civil disobedience. It was seen sublimely in the refusal of Shadrach, Meshach, and Abednego to obey the laws of Nebuchadnezzar because a higher moral law was involved. It was practiced superbly by the early Christians who were willing to face hungry lions and the excruciating pain of chopping blocks before submitting to certain unjust laws of the Roman Empire. To a degree academic freedom is a reality today because Socrates practiced civil disobedience.

We can never forget that everything Hitler did in Germany was "legal" and everything the Hungarian freedom fighters did in Hungary was "illegal." It was "illegal" to aid and comfort a Jew in Hitler's Germany. But I am sure that, if I had lived in Germany during that time, I would have aided and comforted my Jewish brothers even though it was illegal. If I lived in a Communist country today where certain principles dear to the Christian faith are suppressed, I believe I would openly advocate disobeying these anti-religious laws.[5]

I must make two honest confessions to you, my Christian and Jewish brothers. First I must confess that over the last few years I have been gravely disappointed with the white moderate. I have almost reached the regrettable conclusion that the Negroes' great stumbling block in the stride toward freedom is not the White Citizens' "Counciler" or the Ku Klux Klanner, but

[4] What distinctions does King make between just and unjust laws? Does he make a reasonable case for breaking unjust laws?

[5] Would King's audience be likely to accept his contentions that the breaking of certain laws would be all right in the three societies he refers to here?

the white moderate who is more devoted to "order" than to justice; who prefers a negative peace which is the absence of tension to a positive peace which is the presence of justice; who constantly says "I agree with you in the goal you seek, but I can't agree with your methods of direct action"; who paternalistically feels that he can set the timetable for another man's freedom; who lives by the myth of time and who constantly advises the Negro to wait until a "more convenient season." Shallow understanding from people of good will is more frustrating than absolute misunderstanding from people of ill will. Lukewarm acceptance is much more bewildering than outright rejection.

I had hoped that the white moderate would understand that law and order exist for the purpose of establishing justice, and that when they fail to do this they become the dangerously structured dams that block the flow of social progress. I had hoped that the white moderate would understand that the present tension in the South is merely a necessary phase of the transition from an obnoxious negative peace, where the Negro passively accepted his unjust plight, to a substance-filled positive peace, where all men will respect the dignity and worth of human personality.

Actually, we who engage in nonviolent direct action are not the creators of tension. We merely bring to the surface the hidden tension that is already alive. We bring it out in the open where it can be seen and dealt with. Like a boil that can never be cured as long as it is covered up but must be opened with all its pus-flowing ugliness to the natural medicines of air and light, injustice must likewise be exposed, with all of the tension its exposing creates, to the light of human conscience and the air of national opinion before it can be cured.

In your statement you asserted that our actions, even though peaceful, must be condemned because they precipitate violence. But can this assertion be logically made? Isn't this like condemning the robbed man because his possession of money precipitated the evil act of robbery? Isn't this like condemning

Socrates because his unswerving commitment to truth and his philosophical delvings precipitated the misguided popular mind to make him drink the hemlock? Isn't this like condemning Jesus because His unique God consciousness and never-ceasing devotion to His will precipitated the evil act of crucifixion? We must come to see, as Federal courts have consistently affirmed, that it is immoral to urge an individual to withdraw his efforts to gain his basic constitutional rights because the quest precipitates violence. Society must protect the robbed and punish the robber.[6]

I had also hoped that the white moderate would reject the myth of time. I received a letter this morning from a white brother in Texas which said: "All Christians know that the colored people will receive equal rights eventually, but is it possible that you are in too great of a religious hurry? It has taken Christianity almost two thousand years to accomplish what it has. The teachings of Christ take time to come to earth." All that is said here grows out of a tragic misconception of time. It is the strangely irrational notion that there is something in the very flow of time that will inevitably cure all ills. Actually time is neutral. It can be used either destructively or constructively. I am coming to feel that the people of ill will have used time much more effectively than the people of good will.

We will have to repent in this generation not merely for the vitriolic words and actions of the bad people, but for the appalling silence of the good people. We must come to see that human progress never rolls in on wheels of inevitability. It comes through the tireless efforts and persistent work of men willing to be co-workers with God, and without this hard work time itself becomes an ally of the forces of social stagnation.

We must use time creatively, and forever realize that the time is always ripe to do right. Now is the time to make real the promise of democracy, and transform our pending national elegy

---

[6] Does the material in this paragraph satisfactorily answer the charge that civil-rights actions, even though peaceful, must be condemned because they precipitate violence?

into a creative psalm of brotherhood. Now is the time to lift our national policy from the quicksand of racial injustice to the solid rock of human dignity.

You spoke of our activity in Birmingham as extreme. At first I was rather disappointed that fellow clergymen would see my nonviolent efforts as those of the extremist. I started thinking about the fact that I stand in the middle of two opposing forces in the Negro community. One is a force of complacency made up of Negroes who, as a result of long years of oppression, have been so completely drained of self-respect and a sense of "some-bodiness" that they have adjusted to segregation, and of a few Negroes in the middle class who, because of a degree of academic and economic security, and because at points they profit by segregation, have unconsciously become insensitive to the problems of the masses. The other force is one of bitterness and hatred and comes perilously close to advocating violence. It is expressed in the various black nationalist groups that are springing up over the nation, the largest and best known being Elijah Muhammad's Muslim movement. This movement is nourished by the contemporary frustration over the continued existence of racial discrimination. It is made up of people who have lost faith in America, who have absolutely repudiated Christianity, and who have concluded that the white man is an incurable "devil."

I have tried to stand between these two forces saying that we need not follow the "do-nothingism" of the complacent or the hatred and despair of the black nationalist. There is the more excellent way of love and nonviolent protest. I'm grateful to God that, through the Negro church, the dimension of non-violence entered our struggle. If this philosophy had not emerged I am convinced that by now many streets of the South would be flowing with floods of blood. And I am further convinced that if our white brothers dismiss us as "rabble rousers" and "outside agitators"—those of us who are working through the channels of nonviolent direct action—and refuse to support our nonviolent efforts, millions of Negroes, out of frustration and despair, will seek solace and security in black nationalist ideologies, a development that will lead inevitably to a frightening racial nightmare.

Oppressed people cannot remain oppressed forever. The urge for freedom will eventually come. This is what has happened to the American Negro. Something within has reminded him of his birthright of freedom; something without has reminded him that he can gain it. Consciously and unconsciously, he has been swept in by what the Germans call the *Zeitgeist*, and with his black brothers of Africa, and his brown and yellow brothers of Asia, South America, and the Caribbean, he is moving with a sense of cosmic urgency toward the promised land of racial justice. Recognizing this vital urge that has engulfed the Negro community, one should readily understand public demonstrations.

The Negro has many pent-up resentments and latent frustrations. He has to get them out. So let him march sometime; let him have his prayer pilgrimages to the city hall; understand why he must have sit-ins and freedom rides. If his repressed emotions do not come out in these nonviolent ways, they will come out in ominous expressions of violence. This is not a threat; it is a fact of history.[7] So I have not said to my people, "Get rid of your discontent." But I have tried to say that this normal and healthy discontent can be channeled through the creative outlet of nonviolent direct action. Now this approach is being dismissed as extremist. I must admit that I was initially disappointed in being so categorized.

But as I continued to think about the matter I gradually gained a bit of satisfaction from being considered an extremist. Was not Jesus an extremist in love? "Love your enemies, bless them that curse you, pray for them that despitefully use you." Was not Amos an extremist for justice—"Let justice roll down like waters and righteousness like a mighty stream." Was not Paul an extremist for the gospel of Jesus Christ—"I bear in my body the marks of the Lord Jesus." Was not Martin Luther an extremist—"Here I stand; I can do none other so help me God." Was not John Bunyan an extremist—"I will stay in jail to the

[7] How can it be historically demonstrated that King is correct here?

end of my days before I make a butchery of my conscience."
Was not Abraham Lincoln an extremist—"This nation cannot
survive half slave and half free." Was not Thomas Jefferson an
extremist—"We hold these truths to be self evident that all
men are created equal."

So the question is not whether we will be extremist but what
kind of extremist will we be. Will we be extremists for hate or
will we be extremists for love? Will we be extremists for the
preservation of injustice—or will we be extremists for the cause
of justice? In that dramatic scene on Calvary's hill three men
were crucified. We must never forget that all three were crucified for the same crime—the crime of extremism. Two were extremists for immorality, and thus fell below their environment.
The other, Jesus Christ, was an extremist for love, truth, and
goodness, and thereby rose above His environment. So, after
all, maybe the South, the nation, and the world are in dire need
of creative extremists.[8]

I had hoped that the white moderate would see this. Maybe
I was too optimistic. Maybe I expected too much. I guess I
should have realized that few members of a race that has oppressed another race can understand or appreciate the deep
groans and passionate yearnings of those that have been oppressed, and still fewer have the vision to see that injustice must
be rooted out by strong, persistent, and determined action. I
am thankful, however, that some of our white brothers have
grasped the meaning of this social revolution and committed
themselves to it. They are still all too small in quantity, but they
are big in quality. Some like Ralph McGill, Lillian Smith, Harry
Golden, and James Dabbs have written about our struggle in
eloquent, prophetic, and understanding terms. Others have
marched with us down nameless streets of the South. They have
languished in filthy, roach-infested jails, suffering the abuse and
brutality of angry policemen who see them as "dirty nigger
lovers." They, unlike so many of their moderate brothers and
sisters, have recognized the urgency of the moment and sensed

[8] Does King's identifying himself as an "extremist" damage his *ethos*?

the need for powerful "action" antidotes to combat the disease of segregation.

Let me rush on to mention my other disappointment. I have been so greatly disappointed with the white Church and its leadership. Of course there are some notable exceptions. I am not unmindful of the fact that each of you has taken some significant stands on this issue. I commend you, Rev. Stallings, for your Christian stand on this past Sunday, in welcoming Negroes to your worship service on a non-segregated basis. I commend the Catholic leaders of this state for integrating Springhill College several years ago.

But despite these notable exceptions I must honestly reiterate that I have been disappointed with the Church. I do not say that as one of those negative critics who can always find something wrong with the Church. I say it as a minister of the gospel, who loves the Church; who was nurtured in its bosom; who has been sustained by its spiritual blessings; and who will remain true to it as long as the cord of life shall lengthen.

I had the strange feeling when I was suddenly catapulted into the leadership of the bus protest in Montgomery several years ago that we would have the support of the white Church. I felt that the white ministers, priests, and rabbis of the South would be some of our strongest allies. Instead, some have been outright opponents, refusing to understand the freedom movement and misrepresenting its leaders; all too many others have been more cautious than courageous and have remained silent behind the anesthetizing security of stained glass windows.

In spite of my shattered dreams of the past, I came to Birmingham with the hope that the white religious leadership of this community would see the justice of our cause and, with deep moral concern, serve as the channel through which our just grievances could get to the power structure. I had hoped that each of you would understand. But again I have been disappointed.

I have heard numerous religious leaders of the South call upon their worshippers to comply with a desegregation decision because it is the law, but I have longed to hear white ministers say follow this decree because integration is morally right and the Negro is your brother. In the midst of blatant injustices inflicted upon the Negro, I have watched white churches stand on the sideline and merely mouth pious irrelevancies and sanctimonious trivialities. In the midst of a mighty struggle to rid our nation of racial and economic injustice, I have heard so many ministers say, "Those are social issues with which the Gospel has no real concern," and I have watched so many churches commit themselves to a completely other-worldly religion which made a strange distinction between body and soul, the sacred and the secular.

So here we are moving toward the exit of the twentieth century with a religious community largely adjusted to the *status quo*, standing as a tail light behind other community agencies rather than a headlight leading men to higher levels of justice.

I have traveled the length and breadth of Alabama, Mississippi, and all the other Southern states. On sweltering summer days and crisp autumn mornings I have looked at her beautiful churches with their spires pointing heavenward. I have beheld the impressive outlay of her massive religious education buildings. Over and over again I have found myself asking: "Who worships here? Who is their God? Where were their voices when the lips of Governor Barnett dripped with words of interposition and nullification? Where were they when Governor Wallace gave the clarion call for defiance and hatred? Where were their voices of support when tired, bruised, and weary Negro men and women decided to rise from the dark dungeons of complacency to the bright hills of creative protest?"

Yes, these questions are still in my mind. In deep disappointment, I have wept over the laxity of the Church. But be assured that my tears have been tears of love. There can be no deep disappointment where there is not deep love. Yes, I love the Church; I love her sacred walls. How could I do otherwise? I am in the rather unique position of being the son, the grandson, and the great grandson of preachers. Yes, I see the Church as the body of Christ. But, oh! How we have blemished and scarred that body through social neglect and fear of being nonconformist.

There was a time when the Church was very powerful. It was during that period when the early Christians rejoiced when they were deemed worthy to suffer for what they believed. In those days the Church was not merely a thermometer that recorded the ideas and principles of popular opinion; it was a thermostat that transformed the mores of society. Wherever the early Christians entered a town the power structure got disturbed and immediately sought to convict them for being "disturbers of the peace" and "outside agitators." But they went on with the conviction that they were a "colony of heaven" and had to obey God rather than man. They were small in number but big in commitment. They were too God-intoxicated to be "astronomically intimidated." They brought an end to such ancient evils as infanticide and gladiatorial contest.

Things are different now. The contemporary Church is so often a weak, ineffectual voice with an uncertain sound. It is so often the arch-supporter of the *status quo*. Far from being disturbed by the presence of the Church, the power structure of the average community is consoled by the Church's silent and often vocal sanction of things as they are.

But the judgment of God is upon the Church as never before. If the Church of today does not recapture the sacrificial spirit of the early Church, it will lose its authentic ring, forfeit the loyalty of millions, and be dismissed as an irrelevant social club with no meaning for the twentieth century. I am meeting young people every day whose disappointment with the Church has risen to outright disgust.[9]

Maybe again I have been too optimistic. Is organized religion too inextricably bound to the *status quo* to save our nation and the world? Maybe I must turn my faith to the inner spiritual Church, the church within the Church, as the true *ecclesia* and the hope of the world. But again I am thankful to God that

[9] What are King's "criticisms" of the "white Church and its leadership"? Why does he devote so much of the letter to a discussion of his disappointment with "the white Church"?

some noble souls from the ranks of organized religion have broken loose from the paralyzing chains of conformity and joined us as active partners in the struggle for freedom.

They have left their secure congregations and walked the streets of Albany, Georgia, with us. They have gone through the highways of the South on torturous rides for freedom. Yes, they have gone to jail with us. Some have been kicked out of their churches and lost the support of their bishops and fellow ministers. But they have gone with the faith that right defeated is stronger than evil triumphant. These men have been the leaven in the lump of the race. Their witness has been the spiritual salt that has preserved the true meaning of the Gospel in these troubled times. They have carved a tunnel of hope through the dark mountain of disappointment.

I hope the Church as a whole will meet the challenge of this decisive hour. But even if the Church does not come to the aid of justice, I have no despair about the future. I have no fear about the outcome of our struggle in Birmingham, even if our motives are presently misunderstood. We will reach the goal of freedom in Birmingham and all over the nation, because the goal of America is freedom. Abused and scorned though we may be, our destiny is tied up with the destiny of America.

Before the pilgrims landed at Plymouth, we were here. Before the pen of Jefferson etched across the pages of history the majestic words of the Declaration of Independence, we were here. For more than two centuries our foreparents labored in this country without wages; they made cotton "king"; and they built the homes of their masters in the midst of brutal injustice and shameful humiliation—and yet out of a bottomless vitality they continued to thrive and develop. If the inexpressible cruelties of slavery could not stop us, the opposition we now face will surely fail. We will win our freedom because the sacred heritage of our nation and the eternal will of God are embodied in our echoing demands.

I must close now. But before closing I am impelled to mention one other point in your statement that troubled me profoundly. You warmly commended the Birmingham police force for keeping "order" and "preventing violence." I don't believe you would have so warmly commended the police force if you had seen its angry violent dogs literally biting six unarmed, nonviolent Negroes. I don't believe you would so quickly commend the policemen if you would observe their ugly and inhuman treatment of Negroes here in the city jail; if you would watch them push and curse old Negro women and young Negro girls; if you would see them slap and kick old Negro men and young Negro boys; if you will observe them, as they did on two occasions, refuse to give us food because we wanted to sing our grace together. I'm sorry that I can't join you in your praise for the police department.

It is true that they have been rather disciplined in their public handling of the demonstrators. In this sense they have been rather publicly "nonviolent." But for what purpose? To preserve the evil system of segregation. Over the last few years I have consistently preached that nonviolence demands that the means we use must be as pure as the ends we seek. So I have tried to make it clear that it is wrong to use immoral means to attain moral ends. But now I must affirm that it is just as wrong, or even more so, to use moral means to preserve immoral ends. Maybe Mr. Connor and his policemen have been rather publicly nonviolent, as Chief Prichett was in Albany, Georgia, but they have used the moral means of nonviolence to maintain the immoral end of flagrant racial injustice. T. S. Eliot has said that there is no greater treason than to do the right deed for the wrong reason.

I wish you had commended the Negro sit-inners and demonstrators of Birmingham for their sublime courage, their willingness to suffer, and their amazing discipline in the midst of the most inhuman provocation. One day the South will recognize its real heroes. They will be the James Merediths, courageously and with a majestic sense of purpose, facing jeering and hostile mobs and the agonizing loneliness that characterizes the life of the pioneer. They will be old, oppressed, battered Negro women, symbolized in a 72-year-old woman of Montgomery, Alabama, who rose up with a sense of dignity and with her people decided not to ride the segregated buses, and responded to one who inquired about her tiredness with ungrammatical profundity: "My feets is tired, but my soul is rested." They will be young high school and college students, young ministers of the gospel and a host of the elders, courageously and nonviolently sitting in at lunch counters and willingly going to jail for conscience sake. One day the South will know that when these disinherited children of God sat down at lunch counters they were in reality standing up for the best in the American dream and the most sacred values in our Judeo-Christian heritage, and thus carrying our whole nation back to great wells of democracy which were dug deep by the founding fathers in the formulation of the Constitution and the Declaration of Independence.[10]

Never before have I written a letter this long (or should I say a book?). I'm afraid that it is much too long to take your precious time. I can assure you that it would have been much shorter if I had been writing from a comfortable desk, but what else is there to do when you are alone for days in the dull monotony of a narrow jail cell other than write long letters, think strange thoughts, and pray long prayers? [11]

If I have said anything in this letter that is an overstatement of the truth and is indicative of an unreasonable impatience, I beg you to forgive me. If I have said anything in this letter that is an understatement of the truth and is indicative of my having a patience that makes me patient with anything less than brotherhood, I beg God to forgive me.

I hope this letter finds you strong in the faith. I also hope that circumstances will soon make it possible for me to meet each of you, not as an integrationist or a civil rights leader, but as a fellow clergyman and a Christian brother. Let us all hope that the dark clouds of racial prejudice will soon pass away and the deep fog of misunderstanding will be lifted from our fear-

---

[10] What is the rhetorical effect of identifying the Negro demonstrators with the American dream and the Judeo-Christian heritage?

[11] What is your reaction to King's irony here? Where else in this letter has he turned to the use of irony? How does irony function rhetorically?

drenched communities and in some not too distant tomorrow the radiant stars of love and brotherhood will shine over our great nation with all of their scintillating beauty.

> *Yours for the cause of*
> *Peace and Brotherhood,*
>
> M. L. KING, JR.

STUDY QUESTIONS

1. Martin Luther King describes his immediate audience, eight Alabama clergymen, as men of good will whom he will address in patient and reasonable terms. Does the context of the letter reveal these men as possessing good will? In what sense is King's letter patient and reasonable?

2. As the letter progresses, it becomes evident that the audience is not limited to the eight clergymen. Who is the larger audience of King's letter, and in what way is the immediate audience a part of the larger group?

3. What is the effect of King's use of the appeal to revered authority? How does it describe King's own person, the character of the civil-rights movement, the character of his audience? What is the value of King's occasional appeal to the emotions?

4. King remarks that his civil-rights persuasion breaks laws "openly and lovingly." How is this revealed in King's description of civil-rights action?

5. The Negro has often been accused of not "helping himself." In the context of the letter, what happens when he tries to help himself?

6. In what sense does King see the civil-rights movement as a manifestation of *Zeitgeist*, or the spirit of the era?

7. For a background on the events leading up to and surrounding the Birmingham demonstrations of 1963, see Martin Luther King's *Why We Can't Wait* (New York: Harper & Row, 1963). What were some of the events in Birmingham that got nationwide and world-wide attention?

A Debate at
Cornell University

MARCH 7, 1962

James Farmer was born in Marshall, Texas, on January 12, 1920. He received a Bachelor of Divinity degree in 1941, but instead of entering the ministry, he directed his energies toward social action which got him involved in labor, pacifist, and civil-rights organizations. In 1942, he helped organize the first chapter of the Congress of Racial Equality (CORE); he was CORE's first national chairman and was its national director from 1961 to 1966.

Malcolm X (born Malcolm Little) was born in Omaha, Nebraska, on May 19, 1925. When he was twenty-one years old, he was convicted of burglary and sent to prison, where he converted to the Nation of Islam (Black Muslims). In March, 1964, he withdrew from the Black Muslim organization of Elijah Muhammad to organize first the Muslim Mosque, Inc., and later the nonreligious Organization of Afro-American Unity. He was assassinated in New York on February 21, 1965.

JAMES FARMER

When the Freedom Riders[1] left from Montgomery, Alabama, to ride into the conscience of America and into Jackson, Mississippi, there were many persons who said to us, "Don't go into Mississippi, go any place you like, go to the Union of South

[1] In April and May of 1961, James Farmer, as director of CORE organized and participated in the Freedom Rides; he was one of the many Freedom Riders beaten and jailed for their participation.

Africa, but stay out of Mississippi." They said, "What you found in Alabama will be nothing compared to what you will meet in Mississippi." I remember being told a story by one minister who urged us not to go. He said, "Once upon a time there was a Negro who had lived in Mississippi, lived for a long time running from county to county. Finally he left the state, and left it pretty fast, as Dick Gregory would put it, not by Greyhound, but by bloodhound, and he went to Illinois to live, in Chicago. And unable to find a job there, after several weeks of walking the street unemployed, he sat down and asked God what he should do. God said, 'Go back to Mississippi.' He said, 'Lord, you surely don't mean it, you're jesting. You don't mean for me to go back to Mississippi. There is segregation there!' The Lord said, 'Go back to Mississippi.' The man looked up and said, 'Very well, Lord, if you insist, I will do it, I will go. But will you go with me?' The Lord said 'As far as Cincinnati.' "

The Freedom Riders felt that they should go all the way because there is something wrong with our nation and we wanted to try to set it right. As one of the nation's scholars wrote at the turn of the century, "The problem of the twentieth century will be the problem of the color-line, of the relations between the lighter and the darker peoples of the earth, Asia and Africa, in America, and in the islands of the sea." What prophetic words, indeed. We have seen the struggle for freedom all over the world. We have seen it in Asia; we have seen it in the island of the sea; we have seen it in Africa; and we are seeing it in America now. I think the racist theories of Count DeGobineu, Lothrop Stoddard, and the others have set the pattern for a racism that exists within our country. There are theories that are held today, not only by those men and their followers and successors, but by Ross Barnett, John Patterson devotees and followers of the Klan and the White Citizens Councils, and Lincoln Rockwell of the American Nazi Party.

These vicious racist theories hold that Negroes are inferior and whites are superior innately. Ordained by God, so to speak. No more vicious theory has existed in the history of mankind. I would suggest to you that no theory has provided as much hu-

man misery throughout the centuries as the theory of races—
the theories that say some people are innately inferior and that
others are innately superior. Although we have some of those
theories in our country, we also have a creed of freedom and of
democracy. As Pearl Buck put it, "Many Americans suffer from
a split personality. One side of that personality is believing in
democracy and freedom, as much as it is possible for a man so
to believe. The other side of this personality is refusing, just as
doggedly, to practice that democracy and that freedom, in which
he believes." That was the split personality. Gunnar Myrdal, in
his book, *The American Dilemma*, indicated that this was basically a moral problem, and that we have this credo which
Americans hold to, of freedom, and democracy, and equality,
but still we refuse to practice it. Gunnar Myrdal indicated that
this is sorely troubling the American conscience.[2]

All of us are a part of this system, *all* a part of it. We have all
developed certain prejudices, I have mine, you have yours. It
seems to me that it is extremely dangerous when any individual
claims to be without prejudice, when he really does have it. I'm
prejudiced against women drivers. I think they are a menace to
civilization, and the sooner they are removed from the highways,
the safer we will all be, but I know that's nothing but a prejudice. I have seen women drivers who are better drivers than I
am, but does that destroy my prejudice? No. What I do then is
to separate her from the group of women drivers and say, "Why
she is an exception." Or maybe I say she is driving very well
because she feels guilty. She knows that other women in the
past have had accidents, and so she drives cautiously.

I remember several years ago when I was a youth, attending a
church youth conference, and a young fellow from Mississippi
and I became very good friends. The last day of the conference
as we walked along the road he put his arm on my shoulder and
said, "Jim, I have no race prejudice." "No," said I. "Absolutely
not," said he. I raised my eyebrows. "As a matter of fact," he
went on, "I was thirteen years old before I knew I was any better

[2] What evidence is there in American society to indicate this "split personality"?

than a Negro." Well sometimes a supposed absence of racial prejudice runs quite along those lines. Now prejudice is a damaging thing to Negroes. We have suffered under it tremendously. It damages the lives of little children. I remember when I first came into contact with segregation; it was when I was a child in Mississippi when my mother took me downtown, and on the way back this hot July day I wanted to stop and get a Coke, and she told me I couldn't get a Coke, I had to wait until I got home. "Well why can't I, there's a little boy going in," said I. "I bet he's going to get a Coke." He was. "Well why can't I go?" "Because he's white," she said, "and you're colored." It's not important what happened to me, the fact is that the same thing over and over again happens to every mother's child whose skin happens to be dark.

If the damage that is done to Negroes is obvious, the damage that is done to whites in America is equally obvious, for they're prejudiced. I lived in Texas a large part of my life; [I] remember driving through the state, and after dusk had fallen being followed by cars of whites who forced me off the road and said to me, "Don't you know that your kind is not supposed to be in this town after sundown." I wondered what was happening to these people; how their minds were being twisted, as mine and others like me had had our minds twisted by this double-edged sword of prejudice. It is a disease indeed. It is an American disease. It is an American dilemma.[3]

The Nation Suffers for Segregation

The damage to Negroes is psychological, it is also economic. Negroes occupy the bottom of the economic ladder, the poorest jobs, the lowest paying jobs. Last to be hired, and first to be fired, so that today the percentage of unemployed Negroes is twice as high as that of whites. There has been political damage as well. In the South we find that comparatively few Negroes

[3] In terms of persuasion, what is the effect of Farmer's emphasis on the damage prejudice has done not only to black Americans but to white Americans?

are registered to vote. Many are apathetic even when they could register. The percentage who are registered in the North is almost equally as low. As a result, comparatively few Negroes are elected to political office. Thus, the damage to the Negroes, as a result of the disease of segregation, has been psychological, economic, social, and political. I would suggest to you that the same damages have occurred to whites. Psychological damages are obvious. Economic—the nation itself suffers economically, as a result of denying the right of full development to one-tenth of its population. Skills, talents, and abilities are crushed in their cradle, are not allowed to develop. Snuffed out. Thus, the nation's economy has suffered. People who could be producing are instead walking the streets. People who could be producing in better jobs and producing more are kept in the lower jobs, sweeping the floors and serving other persons. The whole nation has been damaged by segregation. Now, all of us share the guilt too. I myself am guilty. I am guilty because I spent half my life in the South. During those years I participated in segregation, cooperated with it, and supported it.

We are all intricately involved in the system of segregation. We have not yet extricated ourselves. Negroes are involved, and guilty, and share the blame to the extent they themselves have, by their deeds and their acts, allowed segregation to go on for so long. I do not believe that guilt is a part of my genes or your genes. It hinges upon the deeds that you have done. If you have supported segregation, then you are guilty. If you continue to support it, then your guilt is multiplied. But that is your guilt, that is mine. We share the guilt for the disease of segregation, and its continued existence. All too long, Negro Americans have put up with the system of segregation, North and South. Incidentally, it is not a Southern problem, it is a Northern one as well. Segregation exists in housing and in jobs and in schools. We have put up with it, have done nothing about it.

The day before the Freedom Riders left Washington, D. C., to ride into the South, I visited my father who was in the hospital on what proved to be his deathbed. I told him I was going on a Freedom Ride into the South. He wanted to know what it was and I told him. "Where are you going?" he asked, and I told him. He said, "Well, I'm glad that you're going, son, and I hope you survive. I realize you may not return, but," said he, "I'm glad you're going because when I was a child in South Carolina and Georgia, we didn't like segregation either, but we thought that's the way things always had to be and the way they always would be, so we put up with it, took part in it, decided to exist and to stay alive. I am glad," said he, "that there are lots of people today who are no longer willing to put up with the evil of segregation, but want to do something about it and know that something can be done." How right he was indeed.[4]

The masses of Negroes are through putting up with segregation; they are tired of it. They are tired of being pushed around in a democracy which fails to practice what it preaches. The Negro students of the South who have read the Constitution, and studied it, have read the amendments to the Constitution, and know the rights that are supposed to be theirs—they are coming to the point where they themselves want to do something about achieving these rights, not [to] depend on somebody else. The time has passed when we can look for pie in the sky, when we can depend upon someone else on high to solve the problem for us. The Negro students want to solve the problem themselves. Masses of older Negroes want to join them in that. We can't wait for the law. The Supreme Court decision in 1954 banning segregated schools has had almost eight years of existence, yet less than 8 percent of the Negro kids are in integrated schools. That is far too slow. Now the people themselves want to get involved, and they are. I was talking with one of the student leaders of the South only last week; he said, "I myself desegregated a lunch counter, not somebody else, not some big man, some powerful man, but me, little me. I walked the picket line and I sat in and the walls of segregation toppled. Now all people can eat there." One young prize fighter was a cell-mate of mine in the prisons of Mississippi as a Freedom Rider; he

---

[4] James Farmer has made greater use of the example, the story, than Malcolm X. What is the rhetorical effect of Farmer's use of such specifics as examples and stories?

had won his last fight and had a promising career. I saw him three weeks ago and asked him, "How are you coming along?" He said, "Not very well, I lost the last fight and I am through with the prize ring. I have no more interest in it. The only fight I want now," said he, " is the freedom fight. Because I, a little man, can become involved in it, and can help to win freedom." So that's what's happening; you see, we are going to do something about freedom now, we are not waiting for other people to do it. The student sit-ins have shown it; we are winning. As a result of one year of the student sit-ins, the lunch counters were desegregated in more than 150 cities. The walls are tumbling down.

Direct Action Brings Results

Who will say that lunch counters, which are scattered all over the country, are not important? Are we not to travel? Picket lines and boycotts brought Woolworth's to its knees. In its annual report of last year, Woolworth's indicated that profits had dropped and one reason for the drop was the nationwide boycott in which many Northern students, including Cornellians, participated. The picketing and the nationwide demonstrations are the reason that the walls came down in the South, because people were in motion with their own bodies, marching with picket signs, sitting in, boycotting, withholding their patronage. In Savannah, Georgia, there was a boycott, in which 99 percent of the Negroes participated. They stayed out of the stores. They registered to vote. The store owners then got together and said, "We want to sit down and talk; gentlemen, you have proved your point. You have proved that you can control Negroes' purchasing power and that you can control their votes. We need no more proof, we are ready to hire the people that you send." Negroes are hired in those stores now as a result of this community-wide campaign. In Lexington, Kentucky, the theaters were opened up by CORE as a result of picketing and boycotting. Some of the theaters refused to admit Negroes, others would let Negroes sit up in the balcony. They boycotted one, picketed the others. In a short period of time, the theater owners sat down to negotiate. All of the theaters there are open now. Using the same technique, they provided scores of jobs in department stores, grocery stores, and more recently as city bus drivers.

Then came the Freedom Rides. Three hundred and twenty-five people were jailed in Jackson, Mississippi, others beaten, fighting for freedom non-violently. They brought down many, many barriers. They helped to create desegregation in cities throughout the South. The ICC [Interstate Commerce Commission] order was forthcoming as a result of the Freedom Rides and a more recent Supreme Court ruling. CORE sent test teams throughout the South after the ICC order went into effect. The test teams found that in hundreds of cities throughout the South, where terminals had been previously segregated, they now were desegregated and Negroes were using them. Mississippi is an exception, except for two cities; Louisiana is an exception, except for one pocket of the state; but by and large the Rides were successful. And then on Route 40. How many Negroes and interracial groups have driven Route 40 to Washington or to New York and carried their sandwiches, knowing that they could not eat between Wilmington and Baltimore. The Freedom Rides there, and some Cornell students participated in those Freedom Rides, brought down the barriers in more than half of those restaurants and each weekend, rides are taking place aimed at the others. By Easter we will have our Easter dinner in any place we choose on Route 40. At least fifty-three out of the eighty are now desegregated. In voter registration projects, we have registered seventeen thousand Negroes in South Carolina, previously unregistered. The politicians, segregationists, it's true, now call up our leaders and say, "I would like to talk to you because I don't believe in segregation as much as my opponent," or, "We would like to sit down and talk," or, "Can you come by my house and let's talk about this thing." Because they are realizing that now they have to be responsible to the votes of Negroes as well as the handful of whites, these are the things that are being done by people themselves in motion. Not waiting for someone else to do it, not looking forward to pie in the sky at some later date, not expecting a power on high to solve the problem for them, but working to solve it themselves and winning.[5]

Integration Repudiates Racist Theories

What are our objectives: segregation, separation? Absolutely not! The disease and the evils that we have pointed to in our American culture have grown out of segregation and its partner, prejudice. We are for integration, which is the repudiation of the evil of segregation. It is a rejection of the racist theories of DeGobineu, Lothrop Stoddard, and all the others. It matters not whether they say that whites are superior to Negroes and Negroes are inferior, or if they reverse the coin and say that Negroes are superior and whites are inferior. The theory is just as wrong, just as much a defiance of history. We reject those theories. We are working for the right of Negroes to enter all fields of activity in American life. To enter business if they choose, to enter the professions, to enter the sciences, to enter the arts, to enter the academic world. To be workers, to be laborers if they choose. Our objective is to have each individual accepted on the basis of his individual merit and not on the basis of his color. On the basis of what he is worth himself.[6]

This has given a new pride to [a] large number of people. A pride to the people in Mississippi, who themselves saw others, white and Negro, joining them in the fight for freedom; forty-one local citizens went into the jails of Mississippi joining the Freedom Riders. They have come out now and they have started their own non-violent Jackson movement for freedom. They are sitting in. They are picketing, they are boycotting, and it is

[5] In this paragraph and the previous paragraph, Farmer lists the successes of the civil-rights movement. Would Malcolm X consider these meaningful? Do you see them as substantial successes?

[6] Is analogizing the "white supremacy" of DeGobineu (1816–1882) and Stoddard (1883–1950) with the "black racism" of the Black Muslims persuasive?

working. In Macomb, Mississippi, local citizens are now seeking to register to vote, some of them registering. In Huntsville, Alabama, as a result of CORE's campaign there (and we are now under injunction), for the past six weeks local Negro citizens have been sitting in every day at lunch counters. One of the white CORE leaders there in Huntsville was taken out of his house at gunpoint, undressed, and sprayed with mustard oil. That's the kind of treatment they have faced, but they will not give up because they know they are right and they see the effects of their efforts; they see it in the crumbling walls in interstate transportation and in other public facilities.

We are seeking an open society, an open society of freedom where people will be accepted for what they are worth, will be able to contribute fully to the total culture and the total life of the nation.

Now we know the disease, we know what is wrong with America, we know now that the CORE position is in trying to right it. We must do it in interracial groups because we do not think it is possible to fight against caste in a vehicle which in itself is a representative of caste. We know that the students are still sitting in, they are still fighting for freedom. What we want, Mr. X, [as] the representative of the Black Muslims and Elijah Muhammad, to tell us today, is what his program is, what he proposes to do about killing this disease. We know the disease, physician, what is your cure? What is your program and how do you hope to bring it into effect? How will you achieve it? It is not enough to tell us that it may be a program of a black state. The Communists had such a program in the thirties and part of the forties, and they dropped it before the fifties as being impractical. So we are not only interested in the terminology. We need to have it spelled out; if we are being asked to follow it, to believe in it, what does it mean? Is it a separate Negro society in each city? As a Harlem, a South Side Chicago? Is it a separate state in one part of the country? Is it a separate nation in Africa, or elsewhere? Then we need to know how is it to be achieved. I assume that before a large part of land could be granted to Negroes or to Jews or to anybody else in the country it would have to be approved by the Senate of the United States.[7]

You must tell us, Mr. X, if you seriously think that the Senate of the United States which has refused or failed for all these years to pass a strong Civil Rights Bill, you must tell us if you really think that this Senate is going to give us, to give you, a black state. I am sure that Senator Eastland would so vote, but the land that he would give us would probably be in the bottom of the sea. After seeing Alabama and Mississippi, if the power were mine, I would give you those states, but the power is not mine, I do not vote in the Senate. Tell us how you expect to achieve this separate black state.

Now it is not enough for us to know that you believe in black businesses, all of us believe that all Americans who wish to go into business should go into business. We must know, we need to know, if we are to appraise your program, the kind of businesses, how they are to be established; will we have a General Motors, a General Electric? Will I be able to manufacture a Farmer Special? Where am I going to get the capital from? You must tell us if we are going to have a separate interstate bus line to take the place of Greyhound and Trailways. You must tell us how this separate interstate bus line is going to operate throughout the country if all of us are confined within one separate state.

You must tell us these things, Mr. X, spell them out. You must tell us also what the relationship will be between the black businesses which you would develop and the total American economy. Will it be a competition? Will it be a rival economy, a dual economy, or will there be cooperation between these two economies? [8]

Our program is clear. We are going to achieve our goals of integration by non-violent direct action on an interracial level with whites and Negroes jointly cooperating to wipe out a

[7] How does Farmer destroy a bit of Malcolm's *ethos* in this paragraph?
[8] What is the rhetorical effect of Farmer's posing question after question for Malcolm to answer?

disease which has afflicted and crippled all of them, white and black alike. The proof of the pudding is the eating. We have seen barriers fall as the result of using these techniques. We ask you, Mr. X, what is your program?

MALCOLM X

In the name of Allah, the Beneficent, the Merciful, to whom all praise is due, whom we forever thank for giving America's twenty million so-called Negroes the most honorable Elijah Muhammad as our leader and our teacher and our guide.

I would point out at the beginning that I wasn't born Malcolm Little. Little is the name of the slave master who owned one of my grandparents during slavery, a white man, and the name Little was handed down to my grandfather, to my father, and on to me. But after hearing the teachings of the honorable Elijah Muhammad and realizing that Little is an English name, and I'm not an Englishman, I gave the Englishman back his name; and since my own had been stripped from me, hidden from me, and I don't know it, I use X; and someday, as we are taught by the honorable Elijah Muhammad, every black man, woman, and child in America will get back the same name, the same language, and the same culture that he had before he was kidnapped and brought to this country and stripped of these things.[9]

I would like to point out in a recent column by James Reston on the editorial page of *The New York Times*, December 15, 1961, writing from London, [that] Mr. Reston, after interviewing several leading European statesmen, pointed out that the people of Europe, or the statesmen in Europe, don't feel that America or Europe has anything to worry about in Russia; that the people in Europe foresee the time when Russia, Europe, and America will have to unite together to ward off the threat of China and the non-white world. And if this same statement was made by a Muslim, or by the honorable Elijah Muhammad,

[9] What rhetorical effect would these two first paragraphs probably have on an audience composed of white American university students?

it would be classified as racist; but Reston who is one of the leading correspondents in this country and writing for one of the most respected newspapers, points out that the holocaust that the West is facing is not something from Russia, but threats of the combined forces of the dark world against the white world.

Why do I mention this? Primarily because the most crucial problem facing the white world today is the race problem. And the most crucial problem facing white America today is the race problem. Mr. Farmer pointed out beautifully and quoted one writer actually as saying that the holocaust that America is facing is primarily still based upon race. This doesn't mean that when people point these things out that they are racist; this means that they are facing the facts of life that we are confronted with today. And one need only to look at the world troubles in their international context, national context, or local context, and one will always see the race problem right there, a problem that it is almost impossible to duck around.

It so happens that you and I were born at a time of great change, when changes are taking place. And if we can't react intelligently to these changes, then we are going to be destroyed. When you look into the United Nations set-up, the way it is, we see that there is a change of power taking place, a change of position, a change of influence, a change of control. Wherein, in the past, white people used to exercise unlimited control and authority over dark mankind, today they are losing their ability to dictate unilateral terms to dark mankind. Whereas, yesterday dark nations had no voice in their own affairs, today, the voice that they exercise in their own affairs is increasing, which means in essence that the voice of the white man or the white world is becoming more quiet every day, and the voice of the non-white world is becoming more loud every day. These are the facts of life and these are the changes that you and I, this generation, have to face up to on an international level, a national level, or a local level before we can get a solution to the problems that confront not only the white man, but problems that confront also the black man, or the non-white man.

When we look at the United Nations and see how these dark nations get their independence—they can out-vote the Western bloc or what is known as the white world—and to the point where up until last year the United Nations was controlled by the white powers, or Western powers, mainly Christian powers, and the secretaryship used to be in the hands of a white European Christian; but now when we look at the general structure of the United Nations we see a man from Asia, from Burma, who is occupying the position of Secretary, who is a Buddhist, by the way, and we find the man who is occupying the seat of President is a Moslem from Africa, namely Tunisia. Just in recent times all of these changes are taking place, and the white man has got to be able to face up to them, and the black man has to be able to face up to them, before we can get our problem solved, on an international level, a national level, as well as on the local level.

In terms of black and white, what this means is that the unlimited power and prestige of the white world is decreasing, while the power and prestige of the non-white world is increasing. And just as our African and Asian brothers wanted to have their own land, wanted to have their own country, wanted to exercise control over themselves and govern themselves—they didn't want to be governed by whites or Europeans or outsiders, they wanted control over something among the black masses here in America. I think it would be mighty naïve on the part of the white man to see dark mankind all over the world stretching out to get a country of his own, a land of his own, an industry of his own, a society of his own, even a flag of his own, it would be mighty naïve on the part of the white man to think that same feeling that is sweeping through the dark world is not going to leap nine thousand miles across the ocean and come into the black people here in this country, who have been begging you for four hundred years for something that they have yet to get.

In the areas of Asia and Africa where the whites gave freedom to the non-whites a transition took place, of friendliness and hospitality. In the areas where the non-whites had to exercise violence, today there is hostility between them and the white man. In this, we learn that the only way to solve a problem that is unjust, if you are wrong, is to take immediate action to correct it. But when the people against whom these actions have been directed have to take matters in their own hands, this creates hostility, and lack of friendliness and good relations between the two.

An Era of Great Change

I emphasize these things to point up the fact that we are living in an era of great change, when dark mankind wants freedom, justice, and equality. It is not a case of wanting integration or separation, it is a case of wanting freedom, justice, and equality.

Now if certain groups think that through integration they are going to get freedom, justice, equality, and human dignity, then well and good, we will go along with the integrationists. But if integration is not going to return human dignity to dark mankind, then integration is not the solution to the problem. And ofttimes we make the mistake of confusing the objective with the means by which the objective is to be obtained. It is not integration that Negroes in America want, it is human dignity. They want to be recognized as human beings. And if integration is going to bring us recognition as human beings, then we will integrate. But if integration is not going to bring us recognition as human beings, then integration [is] "out the window," and we have to find another means or method and try that to get our objectives reached.[10]

The same hand that has been writing on the wall in Africa and Asia is also writing on the wall right here in America. The same rebellion, the same impatience, the same anger that exists in the hearts of the dark people in Africa and Asia is existing in the hearts and minds of twenty million black people in this country who have been just as thoroughly colonized as the

[10] Malcolm X points out here that integration is a means, not an end in itself. Does his argument appear valid?

people in Africa and Asia. Only the black man in America has been colonized mentally, his mind has been destroyed. And today, even though he goes to college, he comes out and still doesn't even know he is a black man; he is ashamed of what he is, because his culture has been destroyed, his identity has been destroyed; he has been made to hate his black skin, he has been made to hate the texture of his hair, he has been made to hate the features that God gave him. Because the honorable Elijah Muhammad is coming along today and teaching us the truth about black people to make us love ourselves instead of realizing that it is you who taught us to hate ourselves and our own kind, you [who] accuse the honorable Elijah Muhammad of being a hate teacher and accuse him of being a racist. He is only trying to undo the white supremacy that you have indoctrinated the entire world with.

I might point out that it makes America look ridiculous to stand up in world conferences and refer to herself as the leader of the free world. Here is a country, Uncle Sam, standing up and pointing a finger at the Portuguese, and at the French, and at other colonizers, and there are twenty million black people in this country who are still confined to second-class citizenship, twenty million black people in this country who are still segregated and Jim-Crowed, as my friend, Dr. Farmer, has already pointed out. And despite the fact that twenty million black people here yet don't have freedom, justice, and equality, Adlai Stevenson has nerve enough to stand up in the United Nations and point the finger at South Africa, and at Portugal, and at some of these other countries. All we say is that South Africa preaches what it practices and practices what it preaches; America preaches one thing and practices another. And we don't want to integrate with hypocrites who preach one thing and practice another.[11]

The good point in all of this is that there is an awakening going on among whites in America today, and this awakening is manifested in this way: two years ago you didn't know that

[11] Would this accusation of white American hypocrisy alienate Malcolm's audience?

there were black people in this country who didn't want to integrate with you; two years ago the white public had been brainwashed into thinking that every black man in this country wanted to force his way into your community, force his way into your schools, or force his way into your factories; two years ago you thought that all you would have to do is give us a little token integration and the race problem would be solved. Why? Because the people in the black community who didn't want integration were never given a voice, were never given a platform, were never given an opportunity to shout out the fact that integration would never solve the problem. And it has only been during the past year that the white public has begun to realize that the problem will never be solved unless a solution is devised acceptable to the black masses, as well as the black bourgeoisie —the upper-class or middle-class Negro. And when the whites began to realize that these integration-minded Negroes were in the minority, rather than in the majority, then they began to offer an open forum and give those who want separation an opportunity to speak their mind too.

Middle-Class Settles for Integration

We who are black in the black belt, or black community, or black neighborhood, can easily see that our people who settle for integration are usually the middle-class so-called Negroes, who are in the minority. Why? Because they have confidence in the white man; they have absolute confidence that you will change. They believe that they can change you, they believe that there is still hope in the American dream. But what to them is an American dream to us is an American nightmare, and we don't think that it is possible for the American white man in sincerity to take the action necessary to correct the unjust conditions that twenty million black people here are made to suffer morning, noon, and night. And because we don't have any hope or confidence or faith in the American white man's ability to bring about a change in the injustices that exist, instead of asking or seeking to integrate into the American society we want to face the facts of the problem the way they are, and separate ourselves. And in separating ourselves this doesn't mean that we are anti-white, or anti-American, or anti-anything.[12] We feel that if integration all these years hasn't solved the problem yet, then we want to try something new, something different, and something that is in accord with the conditions as they actually exist.[13]

The honorable Elijah Muhammad teaches us that there are over 725 million Moslems or Muslims on this earth. I use both words interchangeably. I use the word Moslem for those who can't undergo the change, and I use the word Muslim for those who can. He teaches us that the world of Islam stretches from the China Seas to the shores of West Africa and that the twenty million black people in this country are the lost-found members of the nation of Islam. He teaches us that before we were kidnapped by your grandfathers and brought to this country and put in chains, our religion was Islam, our culture was Islamic, we came from the Muslim world, we were kidnapped and brought here out of the Muslim world. And after being brought here we were stripped of our language, stripped of our ability to speak our mother tongue, and it's a crime today to have to admit that there are twenty million black people in this country who not only can't speak their mother tongue, but don't even know they ever had one. This points up the crime of how thoroughly and completely the black man in America has been robbed by the white man of his culture, of his identity, of his soul, of his self. And because he has been robbed of his self, he is trying to accept your self. Because he doesn't know who he is, now he wants to be who you are. Because he doesn't know what belongs to him, he is trying to lay claim to what belongs to you. You have brain-washed him and made him a monster.

[12] Is Malcolm correct in saying that separatism does not necessarily mean antiwhite or anti-American?

[13] In this paragraph, Malcolm suggests that whereas "integration all these years" has not solved the problem of racism, something new, separatism, will solve the problem. How long, if at all, have we had "integration" in the United States?

He is black on the outside, but you have made him white on the inside. Now he has a white heart and a white brain, and he's breathing down your throat and down your neck because he thinks he's a white man the same as you are. He thinks that he should have your house, that he should have your factory, he thinks that he should even have your school, and most of them even think that they should have your woman, and most of them are after your woman.[14]

So-Called Negroes Are Lost Sheep

The honorable Elijah Muhammad teaches us that the black people in America, the so-called Negroes,[15] are the people who are referred to in the Bible as the lost sheep, who are to be returned to their own in the last days. He says that we are also referred to in the Bible, symbolically, as the lost tribe. He teaches us in our religion that we are those people whom the Bible refers to who would be lost until the end of time. Lost in a house that is not theirs, lost in a land that is not theirs, lost in a country that is not theirs, and who will be found in the last days by the Messiah who will awaken them and enlighten them, and teach them that which they had been stripped of, and then this would give them the desire to come together among their own kind and go back among their own kind.

And this, basically, is why we who are followers of the honorable Elijah Muhammad don't accept integration: we feel that we are living at the end of time, by this, we feel that we are living at the end of the world. Not the end of the earth, but the end of the world. He teaches us that there are many worlds. The planet is an earth, and there is only one earth, but there are many worlds on this earth, the Eastern world and the Western world. There is a dark world and a white world. There is the

[14] Malcolm refers here, as he did earlier in the debate, to white America's destruction of the black man's identity. How is this central to his presentation?
[15] Malcolm refers here, as he did earlier, to the "so-called Negroes." Why does he say "so-called"?

world of Christianity, and the world of Islam. All of these are worlds and he teaches us that when the book speaks of the end of time, it doesn't mean the end of the earth, but it means the end of time for certain segments of people, or a certain world that is on this earth. Today, we who are here in America who have awakened to the knowledge of ourselves, we believe that there is no God but Allah, and we believe that the religion of Islam is Allah's religion, and we believe that it is Allah's intention to spread his religion throughout the entire earth. We believe that the earth will become all Muslim, all Islam, and because we are in a Christian country we believe that this Christian country will have to accept Allah as God, accept the religion of Islam as God's religion, or otherwise God will come in and wipe it out. And we don't want to be wiped out with the American white man, we don't want to integrate with him, we want to separate from him.

Separation Is the Best Solution

The method by which the honorable Elijah Muhammad is straightening out our problem is not teaching us to force ourselves into your society, or force ourselves even into your political, economic, or any phase of your society, but he teaches us that the best way to solve this problem is for complete separation. He says that since the black man here in America is actually the property that was stolen from the East by the American white man, since you have awakened today and realized that this is what we are, we should be separated from you, and your government should ship us back to where we came from, not at our expense, because we didn't pay to come here. We were brought here in chains. So the honorable Elijah Muhammad and the Muslims who follow him, we want to go back to our own people. We want to be returned to our own people.

But in teaching this among our people and the masses of black people in this country, we discover that the American government is the foremost agency in opposing any move by any large number of black people to leave here and go back among our own kind.[16] The honorable Elijah Muhammad's words and work are harassed daily by the FBI and every other government agency which uses various tactics to make the so-called Negroes in every community think that we are all about to be rounded up, and they will be rounded up too if they will listen to Mr. Muhammad; but what the American government has failed to realize, the best way to open up a black man's head today and make him listen to another black man is to speak against that black man. But when you begin to pat a black man on the back, no black man in his right mind will trust that black man any longer. And it is because of this hostility on the part of the government toward our leaving here that the honorable Elijah Muhammad says then, if the American white man or the American government doesn't want us to leave, and the government has proven its inability to bring about integration or give us freedom, justice, and equality on a basis, equally mixed up with white people, then what are we going to do? If the government doesn't want us to go back among our own people, or to our own people, and at the same time the government has proven its inability to give us justice, the honorable Elijah Muhammad says if you don't want us to go and we can't stay here and live in peace together, then the best solution is separation. And this is what he means when he says that some of the territory here should be set aside, and let our people go off to ourselves and try and solve our own problem.

Some of you may say, Well, why should you give us part of this country? The honorable Elijah Muhammad says that for four hundred years we contributed our slave labor to make the country what it is. If you were to take the individual salary or allowances of each person in this audience it would amount to nothing individually, but when you take it collectively all in

[16] What evidence is there that the American government is opposing any move by any large number of black people to go back to Africa? Is Malcolm's contention about the American government's opposition believable? This is important, for he uses it later in the paragraph as one basis of his argument for separation.

one pot you have a heavy load. Just the weekly wage. And if you realize that from anybody who could collect all of the wages from the persons in this audience right here for one month, why they would be so wealthy they couldn't walk. And if you see that, then you can imagine the result of millions of black people working for nothing for 310 years. And that is the contribution that we made to America. Not Jackie Robinson, not Marian Anderson, not George Washington Carver, that's not our contribution; our contribution to American society is 310 years of free slave labor for which we have not been paid one dime. We who are Muslims, followers of the honorable Elijah Muhammad, don't think that an integrated cup of coffee is sufficient payment for 310 years of slave labor.[17]

JAMES FARMER | *Rebuttal*

I think that Mr. X's views are utterly impractical and that his so-called "black state" cannot be achieved. There is no chance of getting it unless it is to be given to us by Allah. We have waited for a long time for God to give us other things and we have found that the God in which most of us happen to believe helps those who help themselves. So we would like you to tell us, Mr. X, just what steps you plan to go through to get this black state. Is it one that is going to be gotten by violence, by force? Is it going to be given to us by the Federal government? Once a state is allocated, then are the white people who happen to live there to be moved out forcibly, or Negroes who don't want to go to your black state [are they] going to be moved in forcibly? And what does this do to their liberty and freedom?

Now Mr. X suggests that we Negroes or so-called Negroes, as he puts it, ought to go back where we came from. You know, this is a very interesting idea. I think the solution to many of the problems, including the economic problem of our country,

[17] In what sense is Malcolm using "an integrated cup of coffee"?

would be for all of us to go back where we came from and leave the country to the American Indians. As a matter of fact, maybe the American Indian can go back to Asia, where I understand the anthropologists tell us he came from, and I don't know who preceded him there. But if we search back far enough I am sure that we can find some people to people or populate this nation. Now the overwhelming number of Negroes in this country consider it to be their country; their country more than Africa: I was in Africa three years ago, and while I admire and respect what is being done there, while there is certainly a definite sense of identification and sympathy with what is going on there, the fact is that the cultures are so very different. Mr. X, I am sure that you have much more in common with me or with several people whom I see sitting here than you do with the Africans, than you do with Tom Mboya. Most of them could not understand you, or you they, because they speak Swahili or some other language and you would have to learn those languages.

I tell you that we are Americans. This is our country as much as it is white American. Negroes came as slaves, most of us did. Many white people came as indentured servants; indentured servants are not free. Don't forget it wasn't all of you who were on that ship, the Mayflower.

Now separation of course has been proposed as the answer to the problem, rather than integration. I am pleased however that Malcolm, oh pardon me, Mr. X, indicated that if integration works, and if it provides dignity, then we are for integration. Apparently he is almost agreeing with us there. He is sort of saying as King Agrippa said to St. Paul, "Almost thou persuadest me." I hope that he will be able to come forth and make the additional step and join me at the integrationist side of this table. In saying that separation really is the answer and the most effective solution to this problem, he draws a distinction between separation and segregation, saying that segregation is forced ghettoism while separation is voluntary ghettoism. Well now, I would like to ask Mr. X whether it would be voluntary for Negroes to be segregated as long as we allow discrimination in housing throughout our country to exist. If you live in a black state and cannot get a house elsewhere, then are you voluntarily separated, or are you forcibly segregated?

Black Men and White Women

Now Mr. X suggests that actually the Negroes of this country want the white man's women. Now this is a view, of course, which is quite familiar to you; I've heard it before, there are some Negroes who are married to white people, and I, just before I came up, was looking for a back issue of the paper of the Muslims and saw in there an indication that I myself have a white wife. And it was suggested that therefore I have betrayed my people in marrying a white woman. Well you know I happen to have a great deal of faith in the virtues and the abilities and capacities of Negroes. Not only Negroes, but all of the people too. In fact, I have so much faith in the virtues of Negroes that I do not even think those virtues are so frail that they will be corrupted by contact with other people.

Mr. X also indicated that Negroes imitate whites. It is true, we do, he is right. We fix our hair and try to straighten it; I don't do mine, I haven't had a conk in my life, I think they call it a process, now, etc. But this is a part of the culture of course. After the black culture was taken away from us, we had to adopt the culture that was here, adopt it, and adapt to it. But it is also true that white people try to imitate Negroes, with their jazz, with their hair curlers, you know, and their man-tans. I think, Mr. X, that perhaps the grass is always greener on the other side of the fence. Now when we create integration, perhaps it won't be so necessary for us to resort to these devices.

The black bourgeoisie—is it only the middle class that wants integration? Were the sit-in students black bourgeoisie? They didn't fit into the definition in E. Franklin Frazier's book on the black bourgeoisie. Quite to the contrary, these students were lower class people. Many of them were workers working to stay in school. In the Freedom Rides, were they black bourgeoisie? No, we didn't have exceptions there, we had some people who were unemployed. These are not the black bourgeoisie who want integration. Quite to the contrary, very frequently, the middle class developed a vested interest in the maintenance of segregation. Because if they have a store, and if segregation is eliminated, then I'll be in open competition with the white stores. And thus it is most often true, as Frazier pointed out in his book, that the middle class tends to be opposed to desegregation. Now I would wonder also in the building of black businesses if we are not going to be building another black bourgeoisie? If Negroes may not perhaps be giving up one master for another, a white one for a black one? Are we going to build a new Negro middle class and say that no matter how tyrannical it may prove to be it is my own and, therefore, I like it?

Now we of course know that the Negro is sick, the white man is sick, we know that psychologically we have been twisted by all of these things; but still, Mr. X, you have not told us what the solution is except that it is separation, in your view. You have not spelled it out. Well, now, this sickness, as I tried to indicate in my first presentation, springs from segregation. It is segregation that produces prejudice, as much as prejudice produces segregation. In Detroit, at the time of the race riot, the only rioting, the only fighting, was in the all-Negro and all-white sections of the city, where separation was complete. In those several sections of the city where Negroes and whites lived together, next door to each other, there was no fighting because there the people were neighbors or friends. Now you propose separation as the solution to this problem, as the cure to the disease. Here we have a patient that is suffering from a disease caused by mosquitoes, and the physician proposes as a cure that the man go down and lie in a damp swamp and play with wiggletails.[18]

---

[18] Is Farmer's rebuttal a rebuttal in the sense that he refutes or contradicts the contentions made by Malcolm X?

MALCOLM X | *Rebuttal*

I hadn't thought, or intended anyway, to get personal with Mr. Farmer in mentioning his white wife; I thought that perhaps it would probably have been better left unsaid, but it's better for him to say than for me to say it, because then you would think I was picking on him. I think you will find if you were to have gone into Harlem a few years back you would have found on the juke boxes records by Belafonte, Eartha Kitt, Pearl Bailey; all of these persons were very popular singers in the so-called Negro community a few years back. But since Belafonte divorced Marguerite and married a white woman it doesn't mean that Harlem is anti-white, but you can't find Belafonte's records there; or maybe he just hasn't produced a hit. All of these entertainers who have become involved in intermarriage, and I mean Lena Horne, Eartha Kitt, Sammy Davis, Belafonte, they have a large white following, but you can't go into any Negro community across the nation and find records by these artists that are hits in the so-called Negro community. Because, subconsciously, today the so-called Negro withdraws himself from the entertainers who have crossed the line. And if the masses of black people won't let a Negro who is involved in an intermarriage play music for him, he can't speak for him.

The only way you can solve the race problem as it exists is to take into consideration the feelings of the masses, not the minority; the majority, not the minority. And it is proof that the masses of white people don't want Negroes forcing their way into their neighborhood and the masses of black people don't think it's any solution for us to force ourselves into the white neighborhood, so the only ones who want integration are the Negro minority, as I say, the bourgeoisie and the white minority, the so-called white liberals. And the same white liberal who professes to want integration whenever the Negro moves to his neighborhood, he is the first one to move out. And I was talking with one today who said he was a liberal and I asked him where did he live, and he lived in an all-white neighborhood and probably might for the rest of his life. This is conjecture, but I think it stands true. The Civil War was fought one hundred years ago, supposedly to solve this problem. After the Civil War was fought, the problem still existed. Along behind that, the Thirteenth and Fourteenth Amendments were brought about in the Constitution supposedly to solve the problem; after the Amendments, the problem was still right here with us.[19]

Most Negroes think that the Civil War was fought to make them citizens; they think that it was fought to free them from slavery because the real purpose of the Civil War is clothed in hypocrisy. The real purpose of the Amendments is clothed in hypocrisy. The real purpose behind the Supreme Court Desegregation decision was clothed in hypocrisy. And any time integrationists, NAACP, CORE, Urban League, or what have you, will stand up and tell me to spell out how we are going to bring about separation, and here they are integrationists, a philosophy which is supposed to have the support of the Senate, Congress, President, and the Supreme Court, and still with all of that support and hypocritical agreeing, eight years after the desegregation decision, you still don't have what the Court decided on.

So we think this, that when whites talk integration they are being hypocrites, and we think that the Negroes who accept token integration are also being hypocrites, because they are the only ones who benefit from it, the handful of hand-picked, high-class, middle-class Uncle Tom Negroes. They are hand-picked by whites and turned loose in a white community and they're satisfied. But if all of the black people went into the white community, overnight you would have a race war. If four or five little black students going to school in New Orleans bring about the riots that we saw down there, what do you think would happen if all of the black people tried to go to any school that they want, you would have a race war. So our approach to it, those of us who follow the honorable Elijah Muhammad, we feel that it is more sensible than running around here waiting for the whites to allow us inside their attic or inside their basement.

[19] How has Malcolm changed the meaning of "problem" in this paragraph?

Anti-Discrimination Groups Discriminate

Every Negro group that we find in the Negro community that is integrated is controlled by the whites who belong to it, or it is led by the whites who belong to it. NAACP has had a white president for fifty-three years, it has been in existence for fifty-three years; Roy Wilkins is the executive secretary, but Spingarn, a white man, has been the president for the past twenty-three years, and before him, his brother, another white man, was president. They have never had a black president. Urban League, another so-called Negro organization, doesn't have a black president, it has a white president. Now this doesn't mean that that's racism, it only means that the same organizations that are accusing you of practicing discrimination, when it comes to the leadership they're practicing discrimination themselves.

The honorable Elijah Muhammad says, and points out to us that in this book (*Anti-Slavery*) written by a professor from the University of Michigan, Dwight Lowell Dumond, a person who is an authority on the race question or slave question, his findings were used by Thurgood Marshall in winning the Supreme Court Desegregation decision. And in the preface of this book, it says that second-class citizenship is only a modified form of slavery. Now I'll tell you why I'm dwelling on this; everything that you have devised yourself to solve the race problem has been hypocrisy, because the scientists who delved into it teach us or tell us that second-class citizenship is only a modified form of slavery, which means the Civil War didn't end slavery and the Amendments didn't end slavery. They didn't do it because we still have to wrestle the Supreme Court and the Congress and the Senate to correct the hypocrisy that's been practiced against us by whites for the past umteen years.

And because this was done, the American white man today subconsciously still regards that black man as something below himself. And you will never get the American white man to accept the so-called Negro as an integrated part of his society until the image of the Negro the white man has is changed, and until the image that the Negro has of himself is also changed.[20]

STUDY QUESTIONS

1. The concepts of integration and separatism are both closely related to the Negro's search for identity. How do Malcolm X and James Farmer treat the origin, manifestation, and solution to this "identity problem" through the content and style of their arguments?

2. Malcolm's argument reveals a shift in tone. At what point does that shift occur? How is the tone determined by content?

3. How does Farmer's frequent use of the "human-interest story" help his argument for integration? How does his appeal to famous names reveal his interest in integration? Why does Malcolm X generally neglect such devices?

4. Farmer and Malcolm X are talking to each other and indirectly to an audience of Cornell University students. What, if any, is the effect of these two audiences on the speakers' arguments? Who attempts more of a dialogue? What devices are used to establish rapport? How is rapport destroyed by the opponent's reaction or lack of reaction?

5. Whose arguments would be more agreeable to the white racist? In what way are both arguments either similar to or divergent from the concept of "black power"?

6. See James Farmer's *Freedom—When?* (New York: Random House, 1965), especially the chapter entitled "Black Nationalists and White Liberals." What does Farmer say about the reaction of most Negroes to the black nationalists' contention that "as a first order of business, before economic or social reforms . . . we must mend black souls and replace shame with pride"? After reading this chapter in Farmer's book, does it appear that Malcolm X and James Farmer are as far apart as their debate at Cornell University seems to indicate? Explain.

7. C. Eric Lincoln in *The Black Muslims in America* (Boston: Beacon, 1961) states that the Black Muslims are, in contrast to the NAACP and the National Urban League, a mass movement. Lincoln devotes a chapter to the means used by the Black Muslims to reach the masses. What are those means and how effective are they?

8. See Malcolm Little's *Autobiography of Malcolm X* (New York: Grove, 1965) and also his *Malcolm X Speaks* (New York: Grove, 1965) for more

[20] Does Malcolm's concluding paragraph indicate that he sees integration as a remote possibility? Has he attempted, in his rebuttal, to answer the numerous questions posed by Farmer? In terms of persuasion, do Malcolm's answers, or the lack of them, appear satisfactory for the occasion?

background on the Black Muslims' and Malcolm's views on race, civil rights, and the black–white relationship in the United States. Do the thoughts and feelings Malcolm expresses in his autobiography and speeches jibe with what he said in his debate with James Farmer? What part of Malcolm's philosophy has been rejected by other civil-rights leaders?

Keynote Address to the NAACP Annual Convention, Los Angeles

JULY 5, 1966

Roy Wilkins was born in St. Louis, Missouri, on August 30, 1901. He received a B.A. degree from the University of Minnesota in 1923 and became a journalist. From 1934 to 1949, he was editor of *Crisis*, the official magazine of the National Association for the Advancement of Colored People (NAACP). He has been executive secretary of the NAACP since April, 1955.

In the transition period of the civil rights movement, 1966 is developing into a critical year. The 57th annual convention of our NAACP is thus a gathering of more than ordinary significance.

All about us are alarums and confusions as well as great and challenging developments. Differences of opinion are sharper. For the first time since several organizations began to function where only two had functioned before, there emerges what seems to be a difference in goals.

Heretofore there were some differences in methods and in emphases, but none in ultimate goals. The end was always to be the inclusion of the Negro American, without racial discrimination, as a full-fledged equal in all phases of American citizenship. The targets were whatever barriers, crude or subtle, which blocked the attainment of that goal.

There has now emerged, first, a strident and threatening

challenge to a strategy widely employed by civil rights groups, namely, nonviolence. One organization, which has been meeting in Baltimore, has passed a resolution declaring for defense of themselves by Negro citizens if they are attacked.

This position is not new as far as the NAACP is concerned. Historically our Association has defended in courts those persons who have defended themselves and their homes with firearms. Extradition cases are not as frequent or as fashionable as they once were, but in past years we have fought the extradition of men who had used firearms to defend themselves when attacked.

We freed seventy-nine Arkansas sharecroppers in a four-year court battle beginning in 1919. They had returned gunfire directed at a meeting they were holding in a church.

We employed the late Clarence Darrow in 1926 to defend a man and his family when a member of a mob threatening his newly-purchased Detroit home was shot and killed. The NAACP has subscribed to nonviolence as a humane as well as a practical necessity in the realities of the American scene, but we have never required this as a deep personal commitment of our members. We never signed a pact either on paper or in our hearts to turn the other cheek forever and ever when we were assaulted.

But neither have we couched a policy of manly resistance in such a way that our members and supporters felt compelled to maintain themselves in an armed state, ready to retaliate instantly and in kind whenever attacked. We venture the observation that such a publicized posture could serve to stir counter-planning, counter-action and possible conflict. If carried out literally as instant retaliation, in cases adjudged by aggrieved persons to have been grossly unjust, this policy could produce—in extreme situations—lynchings, or, in better-sounding phraseology, private, vigilante vengeance.

Moreover, in attempting to substitute for derelict law enforcement machinery, the policy entails the risk of a broader, more indiscriminate crackdown by law officers, under the ready-made excuse of restoring law and order.

It seems reasonable to assume that proclaimed protective vio-

lence is as likely to encourage counter-violence as it is to dis-
courage violent persecution.[1]

But the more serious division in the civil rights movement is
the one posed by a word formulation that implies clearly a difference in goals.

No matter how endlessly they try to explain it, the term
"black power" means anti-white power. In a racially pluralistic
society, the concept, the formation and the exercise of an eth-
nically-tagged power, means opposition to other ethnic powers,
just as the term "white supremacy" means subjection of all non-
white people. In the black–white relationship, it has to mean
that every other ethnic power is the rival and the antagonist of
"black power." It has to mean "going-it-alone." It has to mean
separatism.

Now, separatism, whether on the rarefied debate level of
"black power" or on the wishful level of a secessionist Freedom
City in Watts, offers a disadvantaged minority little except the
chance to shrivel and die.

The only possible dividend of "black power" is embodied in
its offer to millions of frustrated and deprived and persecuted
black people of a solace, a tremendous psychological lift, quite
apart from its political and economic implications.

Ideologically it dictates "up with black and down with white"
in precisely the same fashion that South Africa reverses that
slogan.

It is a reverse Mississippi, a reverse Hitler, a reverse Ku Klux
Klan.

If these were evil in our judgment, what virtue can be claimed
for black over white? If, as some proponents claim, this concept
instills pride of race, cannot this pride be taught without preaching hatred or supremacy based upon race? [2]

Though it be clarified and clarified again, "black power" in

---

[1] How much weight would Wilkins' assumption carry with his audience?

[2] Has Wilkins established that black power or separatism means preaching
hatred or supremacy based upon race? How much supremacy and hatred
was advocated by Malcolm X in his Cornell University debate with James
Farmer?

the quick, uncritical and highly emotional adoption it has received from some segments of a beleaguered people can mean in the end only black death. Even if, through some miracle, it should be enthroned briefly in an isolated area, the human spirit, which knows no color or geography or time, would die a little, leaving for wiser and stronger and more compassionate men the painful beating back to the upward trail.

We of the NAACP will have none of this. We have fought it too long. It is the ranging of race against race on the irrelevant basis of skin color. It is the father of hatred and the mother of violence.

It is the wicked fanaticism which has swelled our tears, broken our bodies, squeezed our hearts and taken the blood of our black and white loved ones. It shall not now poison our forward march.[3]

We seek, therefore, as we have sought these many years, the inclusion of Negro Americans in the nation's life, not their exclusion. This is our land, as much so as it is any American's— every square foot of every city and town and village. The task of winning our share is not the easy one of disengagement and flight, but the hard one of work, of short as well as long jumps, of disappointments, and of sweet successes.[4]

In our Fight for Freedom we choose:

1. The power and the majesty of the ballot, the participation of free men in their government, both as voters and as honorable and competent elected and appointed public servants. Year in and year out, the NAACP voter registration work has proceeded. No one except the Federal Government has registered more Negro voters in Mississippi than the NAACP. In six weeks last summer more than twenty thousand new names were added by our workers alone, with additional thousands during an intensive renewal last winter. That work is continuing under the leadership of our Mississippi state president, Dr. Aaron Henry,

[3] Is this the "wicked fanaticism" of white Americans, or black Americans, or both?

[4] How effective is Wilkins' appeal to work, "disappointments," and "sweet successes"?

and of our state director, Charles Evers. Later this month a summer task force will be at work in Louisiana. Already our South Carolina NAACP is busy on registration, as is our Alabama organization.

We are aware that a Louisiana young man, born along the Mississippi border, has been named and confirmed as one of the seven governors of the Federal Reserve Bank. We know that his extraordinary ability finally tipped the scales, but we know also, that, without ballot power, he would not even have been on the scales ready to be tipped.

2. We choose employment for our people—jobs not hidden by racial labels or euphemisms, not limited by racial restrictions in access and promotion, whether by employers or organized labor. We commend a growing number of corporations for expanding their employment of Negro applicants in technical and professional posts, but we insist that only the surface has been scratched.

We commend the "good guys" among the trade unions for the improvement in opportunities and advancement for the Negro worker, but we condemn the policies of some unions which have either barred or heavily handicapped the Negro worker. Negro employment is in a crisis stage. The rate of unemployment ranges from twice that of whites to four and five times the white rate in some areas. The answer to the complaint of employers that workers are not trained is to institute in-plant training, just as they have in other shortages. The apprentice training stranglehold must be broken, the racially separate seniority lines, the still-persisting segregated local and the remaining crude segregation in plant facilities must be abolished. The demonstrations before the U.S. Steel Corporation offices and plants under the cooperative leadership of Dr. John Nixon, our Alabama president, and Henry Smith, our Pennsylvania president, had wide and beneficial impact.

The Negro migrant worker, the forgotten man in the employment picture, must have attention.

In the Watts district of Los Angeles last year the unemployment rate was more than 30 per cent, a rate higher than that during the great, nationwide depression of the nineteen-thirties. The Negro teenage rate is nearly 25 per cent as against 13 per cent for white teenagers.

Negro employment is a disaster area demanding the strict enforcement of Title VII of the 1964 Civil Rights Act. The NAACP has filed more than one thousand complaints with the Equal Employment Opportunity Commission and will file more until the law accomplishes what it was enacted to do. As evidence of his continuing concern, Congressman Augustus Hawkins of Los Angeles succeeded in having his bill relating to Federal employment passed by the House as an amendment to Title VII of the 1964 Civil Rights Act.

3. We choose to combat the color line in housing. In one breath our opinion-makers decry the existence of the poverty and filth and crime and degradation of the slums, but in the next they decry low-cost housing and fair housing laws. Here in California the hysteria over whether Negro Americans should live in gullies or be pushed into the sea reached the Proposition 14 stage which the state's highest court has declared unconstitutional. But who cares about the Constitution when a Negro might be enabled to move into the neighborhood? One could think black Americans were men from Mars. Instead, we have been here, side by side with the white folks (some of whom just got here), for 345 years.

They tell us to work hard and save our money, to go to school and prepare ourselves, to be "responsible," to rear and educate our children in a wholesome and directed family atmosphere, to achieve, to "get up in the world."

After we do all this, they look us in the eye and bar us from renting or buying a home that matches our achievements and one in keeping with our aspirations for further advancement.[5]

Some public officials, including mayors of cities, and many

[5] Apparently the black American's efforts to work hard, save his money, and become "responsible" are not enough to prevent housing discrimination against him. How does this jibe with Wilkins' earlier remarks about the NAACP position that the blacks will achieve their goals through work, "disappointments," and "sweet successes"?

candidates for election to public office are not above public double talk and private single talk on this issue. Any candidate who orates about basic Americanism or "the American way," but who hems and haws over fair housing legislation, is no friend of the Negro citizen.

The Administration's civil rights bill of 1966 with its vital section barring discrimination in the rental or sale of housing must be enacted with the amendment, already inserted by the committee, providing for administrative redress as well as court action.

Your Congressmen and Senators are at home until July 11 celebrating Independence Day—Freedom Day for the United States. See them or have your branch officers back home see them in person. Urge them to rub some freedom off on twenty million loyal Americans by voting for a strong civil rights bill. Of course the section on punishing in the Federal courts those who attack civil rights workers must pass. And we must have indemnification for victims.

4. Most of all, we choose to secure unsegregated, high quality public education for ourselves and our children. A new report, made public only last week, is a jolt for anyone who thought the 1954 Supreme Court decision or subsequent legislation solved the problem.

The report says officially and professionally what we have contended all along: that predominantly Negro schools are inferior to those attended largely by whites. Also that the achievement gap widens between the first grade and the twelfth. In other words, the longer our children attend racially segregated schools, the farther they fall behind white children.

And, lest the non-Southerners feel smug, the report found that segregation for both whites and Negroes is more complete in the South, but " is extensive in other regions where the Negro population is concentrated: the urban North, Midwest and West."

The Federal Government, whose Office of Education has made some strong statements, must follow up with a strong enforcement of Title VI of the 1964 law. The empty promises of school officials and the defiance of the whole State of Alabama must not be accepted meekly by Federal officials. The furor over the guidelines issued by HEW is another version of the Dixie bluff on race which has worked so well for so many decades. The guidelines are mild. They are legal and not illegal as Governor Wallace proclaimed to his state's educators. They ask the Southerners to do what is for them a strange thing: obey the school desegregation law. On this point the Federal Government must not yield. The Attorney General and the Department of Justice must back up resolutely the legality of Federal action. There can be no temporizing.

Outside the South the call is for unrelenting activity to wipe out de facto school segregation. Boston, Massachusetts, has proved to be the Mississippi of the North. In fact, in fairness to Mississippi and in consideration of the starting points and traditions of the two places, Boston is *below* Mississippi on this issue. The details, the traps, the methods and the progress will be covered in workshop discussions, but here it must be said that before we can get jobs to earn increased income to buy and rent better homes, before we can contribute to the enrichment of our nation, we must have free access to quality education.

The man who shoots and burns and drowns us is surely our enemy, but so is he who cripples our children for life with inferior public education.

5. We also choose to wrestle with the complex problems of urban life, all of which include an attitude toward and a treatment of millions of Negro citizens. The solution of urban problems will become the solution of living in the last third of our century since more than 70 per cent of Americans now live in urban communities.

If it has been asked once, it has been asked a hundred times: Are we going to have a long, hot summer? The answer has many facets, some extremely complex and difficult. But one quick answer is that the police everywhere can make or break urban racial tensions by their conduct toward minority group citizens.

Last summer you had here an upheaval that shook the world. To many of us who looked from afar, it appeared to be a wild, senseless rampage of hate and destruction. But that was far from the whole truth.

There was powder in Watts, piled up and packed down through the years: wide-scale unemployment, both adult and teenage, slum housing, crowded schools, non-existent health facilities, inadequate transportation and—the Parker police attitude. Everyone was suspect and everyone was subject to harassment in one form or another. The community smoldered under the peculiar brand that police place upon a whole section with their constant sirens, their contemptuous searches, their rough talk, their ready guns and their general "Godalmightiness."

The lesson they and city officials have learned from last year is to seek not correction and improvement, but still more repression. Mayor Yorty and whoever writes his scripts testified in Sacramento in support of a so-called riot-control bill.

The only thing one has to remember about this bill is that it would allow a policeman to judge whether an utterance or an act is an incitement to riot! On his own judgment he could arrest or club or otherwise deter—or shoot—a person whom he (not the law or the courts) deemed to be an inciter of riot. Down the drain goes freedom of speech and down, too, possibly, goes a life.

The McCone Report on the 1965 riot called for "costly and extreme" remedies for Watts, undertaken with a "revolutionary attitude." The answer of the City of Los Angeles was to vote down a hospital bond issue. The answer of Mayor Yorty and of his man, Chief Parker, is a trampling-tough riot-control bill which, if enacted, would loose the police, almost without restraint, upon a populace sick to death—literally—of race control. To blot out any remaining fitful light, one of the gubernatorial candidates, full of disavowals, is the darling of those ultra-conservatives who believe in iron control of what they call "violence in the streets"—their code name for Negroes.

If this is the best that a great city can bring to a hard urban problem, one largely of its own making, then God pity both the whites and the Negroes!

We have no panacea for all these problems. We do not proclaim that what we declare here this week is going to change the course of the whole civil rights movement. We do not know all the answers to the George Wallace problem in Alabama, the James Eastland problem in Mississippi, or to the Boston, Massachusetts, school committee and its Louise Day Hicks problem. We certainly don't know the answers to foreign policy and to tax and interest rate puzzlers.

But in this unsettled time when shifts are the order of the day and when change is in the air, we can sail our NAACP ship "steady as she goes," with more drive to the turbines, more skill at the wheel, but no fancy capers for the sake of capers.

We can follow down into each community the really advanced blueprint of the White House Conference "To Fulfill These Rights," which covered four principal areas: economic security and welfare, education, housing, and the administration of justice.

We can expand and point up the community services of our NAACP branches, each of which is, in reality, a citizenship clinic. Just as medical clinics need specialists to cure physical ills, so our branch clinics should recruit volunteer specialists to diagnose and minister to social ills.

We must involve people in the communities in the solution of our problem—not limiting ourselves to our church or lodge or club group.

We must keep the pressure on our local and state education systems through the employment of every legitimate technique: protests, surveys, discussions, demonstrations, picketing and negotiation. Nothing should be overlooked in fighting for better education. Be persistent and ornery; this will be good for the lethargic educational establishment and will aid the whole cause of public education.

Our branches are at work in their territories. In Baltimore, the NAACP won a case against the police commissioner which the Fourth Circuit Court of Appeals declared revealed the most flagrant police practices ever to come before the court. The Blair County, Pennsylvania, NAACP is busy rooting out the remaining discrimination in public accommodations in Clearfield, Pennsylvania.

The Wilmington, Ohio, NAACP has a program for tutoring adults and drop-outs and has recruited college professors and students and textbooks to make the project effective. The Bay City, Michigan, NAACP also has a tutorial program under way as well as continuous work on industrial employment practices and housing. The Stillwater, Oklahoma, NAACP is active on a child care center project and on high school desegregation.

And the Montgomery County, West Virginia, NAACP, bless its heart, is 112 per cent above last year in membership and 500 per cent above last year in funds raised.

Thirty-one branches found time and funds to be present at the Meredith march rally in Jackson, Mississippi, even though the Association, at the last minute, was insulted by the barring of Charles Evers as an NAACP spokesman.

This is only part of the chronicle of "steady as she goes." In a world where the Mayor of Los Angeles is yelling "riot control," where Rhodesia says "never!" to black representation while in America SNCC raises the chant of black power, where the Federal Government at long last is committed,[6] but both the far right and the far left offer vocal and vicious objection, someone has to drive the long haul toward the group goal of Negro Americans and the larger ideal of our young nation.

Our objective is basically as it was laid down in 1909 by the interracial founders of our NAACP.[7] Back there William Lloyd Garrison expressed the strong feeling that the first NAACP conference "will utter no uncertain sound on any point affecting the

[6] In what sense is the United States government "at long last committed"?
[7] Wilkins says that the 1909 objectives of the NAACP are basically the objectives of the NAACP in 1966. Can these objectives be questioned as 1966 objectives in light of the substantial changes that have taken place over the past half century?

vital subject. No part of it is too delicate for plain speech. The republican experiment is at stake, every tolerated wrong to the Negro reacting with double force upon white citizens guilty of faithlessness to their brothers."

As it was then, so it is today. The republican experiment *is* at stake in 1966. More than that, the dream of a brotherhood in equality and justice is imperiled.

Our fraternity tonight, as it was then, is the fraternity of man, not the white, or brown, or yellow, or black man, but man.[8]

STUDY QUESTIONS

1. What is the rhetorical function for Wilkins to list the achievements of the NAACP at the beginning of his speech?

2. Wilkins argues that "black power" means "going it alone" for the Negro, that it means "separatism." Do you think Wilkins has adequately developed this argument? Do you agree that black power necessarily means separatism? Explain.

3. Would you agree with Wilkins that black power is "a reverse Mississippi, a reverse Hitler, a reverse Ku Klux Klan"? Are there any similarities between black power and white racism? Any differences? Explain.

4. As Wilkins portrays the techniques and goals of the NAACP, does the NAACP appear as an organization actively involved in helping Negroes fulfill their self-interests?

5. What material in the speech indicates that Wilkins is aware that although he may not like black power, he must cope with its appeal to Negroes?

6. Wilkins makes references to the Watts "riot" of 1965. See Robert Conot, *Rivers of Blood, Years of Darkness* (New York: Bantam, 1967), for accounts of the causes of the "riot," the incidents and their results, and for accounts of what has and has not been done in Watts since 1965. Have any recent serious efforts been made to alleviate the problems that contributed to the igniting of the "powder in Watts, piled up and packed down through the years"?

[8] In what ways does the NAACP's program, as outlined by Wilkins, differ from that of CORE's, as suggested by James Farmer in the Cornell University debate?

STOKELY CARMICHAEL

*Power and Racism**

Stokely Carmichael was born in Port-au-Spain, Trinidad, on June 29, 1941. He came with his parents to the United States in 1953 and became a citizen when his parents were naturalized. He attended Howard University and received a B.A. degree in 1964. Mr. Carmichael was chairman of the Student Nonviolent Coordinating Committee (SNCC) from May 1966 to May 1967.

One of the tragedies of the struggle against racism is that up to now there has been no national organization which could speak to the growing militancy of young black people in the urban ghetto. There has been only a civil rights movement, whose tone of voice was adapted to an audience of liberal whites. It served as a sort of buffer zone between them and angry young blacks. None of its so-called leaders could go into a rioting community and be listened to. In a sense, I blame ourselves—together with the mass media—for what has happened in Watts, Harlem, Chicago, Cleveland, Omaha. Each time the people in those cities saw Martin Luther King get slapped, they became angry; when they saw four little black girls bombed to death, they were angrier; and when nothing happened, they were steaming. We had nothing to offer that they could see, except to go out and be beaten again. We helped to build their frustration.[1]

An organization which claims to speak for the needs of a community—as does the Student Nonviolent Coordinating Committee—must speak in the tone of that community, not

* Pamphlet distributed by SNCC, from an originally longer version, "What We Want," in *The New York Review of Books*, 7 (September 22, 1966), pp. 5–8.

[1] Does Carmichael's explanation for the frustrations of the black American clarify, in part, the turning of some blacks to rebellion through violence?

as somebody else's buffer zone. This is the significance of black power as a slogan. For once, black people are going to use the words they want to use—not just the words whites want to hear. And they will do this no matter how often the press tries to stop the use of the slogan by equating it with racism or separatism.

An organization which claims to be working for the needs of a community—as SNCC does—must work to provide that community with a position of strength from which to make its voice heard. This is the significance of black power beyond the slogan.

Black power can be clearly defined for those who do not attach the fears of white America to their questions about it. We should begin with the basic fact that black Americans have two problems: they are poor and they are black. All other problems arise from this two-sided reality: lack of education, the so-called apathy of black men. Any program to end racism must address itself to that double reality.

Almost from its beginning, SNCC sought to address itself to both conditions with a program aimed at winning political power for impoverished Southern blacks. We had to begin with politics because black Americans are a propertyless people in a country where property is valued above all. We had to work for power, because this country does not function by morality, love, and nonviolence, but by power.[2] Thus we determined to win political power, with the idea of moving on from there into activity that would have economic effects. With power, the masses could *make or participate in making* the decisions which govern their destinies, and thus create basic change in their day-to-day lives.

But if political power seemed to be the key to self-determination, it was also obvious that the key had been thrown down a deep well many years earlier. Disenfranchisement, maintained by racist terror, makes it impossible to talk about organizing for political power in 1960. The right to vote had to be won, and SNCC workers devoted their energies to this from 1961 to 1965. They set up voter registration drives in the Deep South. They

[2] Do you accept, for the most part, this contention that "this country does not function by morality, love, and nonviolence, but by power"?

created pressure for the vote by holding mock elections in Mississippi in 1963 and by helping to establish the Mississippi Freedom Democratic Party (MFDP) in 1964. That struggle was eased, though not won, with the passage of the 1965 Voting Rights Act. SNCC workers could then address themselves to the question: "Who can we vote for, to have our needs met—how do we make our vote meaningful?" . . .

In Lowndes County, Alabama, black power will mean that if a Negro is elected sheriff, he can end police brutality. If a black man is elected tax assessor, he can collect and channel funds for the building of better roads and schools serving black people—thus advancing the move from political power into the economic arena. In such areas as Lowndes, where black men have a majority, they will attempt to use it to exercise control. This is what they seek: control. Where Negroes lack a majority, black power means proper representation and sharing of control. It means the creation of power bases from which black people can work to change statewide or nationwide patterns of oppression through pressure from strength—instead of weakness. Politically, black power means what it has always meant to SNCC: the coming-together of black people to elect representatives and *to force those representatives to speak to their needs.*[3] It does not mean merely putting black faces into office. A man or woman who is black and from the slums cannot be automatically expected to speak to the needs of black people. Most of the black politicians we see around the country today are not what SNCC means by black power. The power must be that of a community, and emanate from there. . . .

Ultimately, the economic foundations of this country must be shaken if black people are to control their lives. The colonies of the United States—and this includes the black ghettoes within its borders, north and south—must be liberated. For a century, this nation has been like an octopus of exploitation, its tentacles stretching from Mississippi and Harlem to South America, the Middle East, southern Africa, and Vietnam; the form of exploitation varies from area to area but the essential result has been

[3] Does this definition run contrary to any American political principles?

the same—a powerful few have been maintained and enriched at the expense of the poor and voiceless colored masses. This pattern must be broken. As its grip loosens here and there around the world, the hopes of black Americans become more realistic. For racism to die, a totally different America must be born.

This is what the white society does not wish to face; this is why that society prefers to talk about integration. But integration speaks not at all to the problem of poverty, only to the problem of blackness. Integration today means the man who "makes it," leaving his black brothers behind in the ghetto as fast as his new sports car will take him. It has no relevance to the Harlem wino or to the cotton-picker making three dollars a day. As a lady I know in Alabama once said, "the food that Ralph Bunche eats doesn't fill my stomach."

Integration, moreover, speaks to the problem of blackness in a despicable way. As a goal, it has been based on complete acceptance of the fact that *in order to have* a decent house or education, blacks must move into a white neighborhood or send their children to a white school.[4] This reinforces, among both black and white, the idea that "white" is automatically better and "black" is by definition inferior. This is why integration is a subterfuge[5] for the maintenance of white supremacy. It allows the nation to focus on a handful of Southern children who get into white schools, at great price, and to ignore the 94 per cent who are left behind in unimproved all-black schools. Such situations will not change until black people have power—to control their own school boards, in this case. Then Negroes become equal in a way that means something, and integration ceases to be a one-way street. Then integration doesn't mean draining skills and energies from the ghetto into white neighborhoods; then it can mean white people moving from Beverly Hills into Watts, white people joining the Lowndes County

---

[4] Is Carmichael's contention that "integration" has been and is primarily a "one-way street" persuasively acceptable?

[5] Given Carmichael's assumptions, must his audience agree that "integration is a subterfuge for the maintenance of white supremacy"?

Freedom Organization. Then integration becomes relevant. . . .

To most whites, black power seems to mean that the Mau Mau are coming to the suburbs at night. The Mau Mau are coming, and whites must stop them. Articles appear about plots to "get Whitey," creating an atmosphere in which "law and order must be maintained." Once again, responsibility is shifted from the oppressor to the oppressed. Other whites chide, "Don't forget—you're only 10 per cent of the population; if you get too smart, we'll wipe you out." If they are liberals, they complain, "what about me?—don't you want my help any more?" These are people supposedly concerned about black Americans, but today they think first of themselves, of their feelings of rejection. Or they admonish, "you can't get anywhere without coalitions," when there is in fact no group at present with whom to form a coalition in which blacks will not be absorbed and betrayed. . . .

White America will not face the problem of color, the reality of it. The well-intended say: "We're all human, everybody is really decent, we must forget color." But color cannot be "forgotten" until its weight is recognized and dealt with . . .[6]

The need for psychological equality is the reason why SNCC today believes that blacks must organize in the black community. Only black people can convey the revolutionary idea that black people are able to do things themselves. Only they can help create in the community an aroused and continuing black consciousness that will provide the basis for political strength. In the past, white allies have furthered white supremacy without the whites involved realizing it—or wanting it, I think. Black people must do things for themselves; they must get poverty money they will control and spend themselves, they must conduct tutorial programs themselves so that black children can identify with black people . . .[7]

This does not mean we don't welcome help, or friends. But we want the right to decide whether anyone is, in fact, our

[6] Is the implication here that "color can be forgotten"?

[7] Is there merit to Carmichael's position that black Americans must conduct their own affairs and control their own destiny? Is there a "separatism" implicit here?

friend. In the past, black Americans have been almost the only people whom everybody and his momma could jump up and call their friends. We have been tokens, symbols, objects—as I was in high school to many young whites, who liked having "a Negro friend." We want to decide who is our friend, and we will not accept someone who comes to us and says: "If you do X, Y, and Z, then I'll help you" . . .

I have said that most liberal whites react to black power with the question, What about me?, rather than saying: Tell me what you want me to do and I'll see if I can do it. There are answers to the right question. One of the most disturbing things about almost all white supporters of the movement has been that they are afraid to go into their own communities—which is where the racism exists—and work to get rid of it. They want to run from Berkeley to tell us what to do in Mississippi; let them look instead at Berkeley. They admonish blacks to be non-violent; let them preach nonviolence in the white community. They come to teach me Negro history; let them go to the suburbs and open up freedom schools for whites. Let them work to stop America's racist foreign policy; let them press this government to cease supporting the economy of South Africa.[8]

There is a vital job to be done among poor whites. We hope to see, eventually, a coalition between poor blacks and poor whites. That is the only coalition which seems acceptable to us, and we see such a coalition as the major internal instrument of change in American society. SNCC has tried several times to organize poor whites; we are trying again now, with an initial training program in Tennessee. It is purely academic today to talk about bringing poor blacks and whites together, but the job of creating a poor-white power bloc must be attempted. The main responsibility for it falls upon whites.

. . . our vision is not merely of a society in which all black

[8] Is Carmichael correct in his implication that the focus to eradicate racism has been on the black community and not on the white? What has been done in the white community, the white suburb, the white schools to eradicate racism?

men have enough to buy the good things of life. When we urge that black money go into black pockets, we mean the communal pocket. We want to see money go back into the community and used to benefit it. We want to see the cooperative concept applied in business and banking. We want to see black ghetto residents demand that an exploiting landlord or store keeper sell them, at minimal cost, a building or a shop that they will own and improve cooperatively; they can back their demand with a rent strike, or a boycott, and a community so unified behind them that no one else will move into the building or buy at the store. The society we seek to build among black people, then, is not a capitalist one. It is a society in which the spirit of community and humanistic love prevail. The word love is suspect; black expectations of what it might produce have been betrayed too often. But those were expectations of a response from the white community, which failed us. The love we seek to encourage is within the black community, the only American community where men call each other "brother" when they meet. We can build a community of love only where we have the ability and power to do so: among blacks.

As for white America, perhaps it can stop crying out against "black supremacy," "black nationalism," "racism in reverse," and begin facing reality. The reality is that this nation, from top to bottom, is racist;[9] that racism is not primarily a problem of "human relations" but of an exploitation maintained—either actively or through silence—by the society as a whole. Camus and Sartre have asked, can a man condemn himself? Can whites, particularly liberal whites, condemn themselves? Can they stop blaming us, and blame their own system? Are they capable of the shame which might become a revolutionary emotion?

We have found that they usually cannot condemn themselves, and so we have done it. But the rebuilding of this society, if at all possible, is basically the responsibility of whites—not blacks.

[9] How does this assertion that the United States "from top to bottom is racist" jibe with the findings of the 1968 *Report of the National Advisory Commission on Civil Disorders?*

We won't fight to save the present society, in Vietnam or any-where else. We are just going to work, in the way *we* see fit, and on goals *we* define, not for civil rights but for all our human rights.

STUDY QUESTIONS

1. In light of Carmichael's arguments, how would liberal whites, conserva-tive whites, conservative civil-rights advocates, and radical civil-rights ad-vocates react to the black-power slogan?

2. Though the intended audience of Carmichael's article is liberal and white, Carmichael establishes a barrier between himself and his audience. How does that barrier emphasize Carmichael's argument? What stylistic devices are used to establish the barrier?

3. Both the pamphlet version reprinted here and the original longer ver-sion of it, "What We Want," in *The New York Review of Books*, 7 (September 22, 1966), pp. 5–8, were published as an appeal for funds. Read the original version and try to determine the rhetorical reasons for SNCC's choice of excerpts that constitute the pamphlet version.

4. The American concept of individualism, a concept that can lead to selfishness or self-fulfillment, pervades this selection. Determine Carmi-chael's views of whites and Negroes in light of the concept of individual-ism.

5. For some background information on Carmichael and Robert Penn Warren's interview with Carmichael, see "Two for SNCC," *Commentary*, 39 (April 1965), pp. 38–48. Compare Carmichael's 1965 views with his 1967 views on racism, civil rights, black power, and the black–white rela-tionship in the United States.

6. For some personal background on Carmichael and his work in SNCC, see Lerone Bennett, Jr., "Stokely Carmichael: Architect of Black Power," *Ebony*, 21 (September 1966), pp. 25–32. Trace Carmichael's development into a civil-rights leader.

7. See "Elements of Black Power" in Charles E. Fager, *White Reflections on Black Power* (Grand Rapids, Michigan: William B. Eerdmans Publish-ing Co., 1967). In his defense of black power and SNCC, does Fager present a convincing case? Explain.

STOKELY CARMICHAEL

Speech at
Morgan State College*

JANUARY 16, 1967

Good afternoon. It is good to be back here at Morgan. I used to party here when I was at school—after we sat in in Baltimore on Route 40.

I would hope that some of the people who have been disagreeing with the concept of black power would be here today. I would suggest that they read two articles—one which I wrote for *The New York Review of Books* in September and one that appeared in the *Massachusetts Review* in the fourth quarter of 1966.[1] They explain the theoretical concept of black power, they criticize the exponents of the coalition theory and those who say that integration is the only route to solving the racial problem in this country.

I would think that at a black university it would be absurd for me to talk about black power, but rather to talk to black students about what their role is to be in the coming struggle. And so my remarks today would be addressed to you, black students of Morgan, to give you a chance to hear some of the things that you never hear about. You need to stop being ashamed of being black and come on home.

So that while there are many members of the press here, you should pay them no mind because they will not be able to understand what we are talking about. As to the criticism we have been receiving from the press, I was reading George Bernard

---

* From a taped transcription.

[1] In how many different ways has Carmichael established *ethos* in this paragraph?

Shaw the other night and I came across a sentence which I thought was quite apropos. He said that all criticism is in fact autobiography. So the press ought to dig them some Mr. Shaw.

We want to level, before we begin, against several people at this university who, in October, when we were supposed to speak, canceled the speech. Now we understand there were all sorts of bureaucratic tie-ups for canceling the speech. We know that elections were close at hand in Maryland and there was a feeling that—on my part, I am not saying that anyone really said this—that the people were scared, and so they canceled the speech. They were scared that if I spoke here, Mahoney would win. Now one of the reasons I want to talk about that is that I think it is important to understand what that means. What I think the country is trying to do is to kill the free speech of the Student Nonviolent Coordinating Committee.[2]

So that in the beginning I would like to read from one of my favorite men—Frederick Douglass—I hope he is yours. You know Baltimore was his home spot, where he spent his early age. It was from Baltimore that he escaped to freedom. I want to read it because I think it is crystal clear in our minds what we must do in this generation to move for black power. Our mothers scrubbed floors. Our fathers were Uncle Toms. They didn't do that so we could scrub floors and be Uncle Toms. They did it so that this generation can fight for black power and that is what we are about to do and that is what you ought to understand. Mr. Douglass said,

Those who profess to favor freedom yet deprecate agitation are men who want crops without plowing up the ground; they want rain without thunder and lightning. They want the ocean without the awful roar of its many waters. . . . Power concedes nothing without demand. It never did and it never will. Find out just what any people will quietly submit to and you have found out the exact measure of injustice and wrong which will be imposed upon them,

[2] Would an audience of college students be more likely or less likely interested in a speaker who has been previously banned from speaking on their campus?

and these will continue till they are resisted with either words or blows, or with both. The limits of tyrants are prescribed by the endurance of those whom they oppress.

Following in Mr. Douglass's footsteps,[3] we intend to strike our first blow for our liberation, and we will let the chips fall where they may. We do not wish to earn the good will of anybody who is oppressing us. They should rather try to earn our good will since they have been oppressing us.

Now we ought to then outline the points we want to discuss. We want to talk about what this country has been able to do to black people. What it has been able to do is to make us ashamed of being black. And that is one of the first recognitions of a free people. That we recognize that we must be united as a people, that we understand the concept of peoplehood and not be ashamed of ourselves. That means that we must stop imitating white society and begin to create for ourselves and our own and begin to embody our own cultural patterns so that we will be holding dear to those things which we have created.

For example, it is nonsensical for black people to have debutante balls. It is nonsensical because you are imitating that which white society has given to you and which you know nothing about. Wouldn't it be better to take that $500 and give it to Morgan so that you could begin to develop a good black institution?

Now imitation runs deep in the black community in this country. It runs very deep. You know when we first got people to go to college and they went to the first white university in this country, there were things called fraternities and sororities. We are going to talk about it.

Now what happened was that our black brothers and sisters could not get into these fraternities. They kept them out because of the color of their skin. So what did our brothers do—they turned around and formed something called Kappas, and only light-skinned Negroes could get in. Our black sisters, not

[3] How does Carmichael help his persuasive efforts by this reference to Douglass?

to be outdone, formed AKA for only bluebloods. So the other dark-skinned brothers, not to be outdone, set up Omega and Alpha. And then, of course, we had the counterparts, the Deltas.[4] Now, wouldn't it have been far better if those people, instead of imitating a society which had been built on exclud-ing them, had turned around and built a fraternity which would have included everybody? Perhaps that is the greatest problem which you as black students face. You are never asked to create, only to imitate.

The philosophers [Albert] Camus and [Jean Paul] Sartre raised the question of self-condemnation in most of their writ-ings. Camus, you know, is an existentialist. He wrote *The Rebel*, *The Stranger*. You ought to read them. What Camus says is that self-condemnation is impossible. And we in SNCC agree with that. Self-condemnation is impossible.

There are examples of that. For example, there were Nazi prisoners during World War II. Those who were captured. If they admitted that they had killed six million Jews, they had to commit suicide. They must commit suicide. The ones who were able to live were the ones who had said, "We did not kill six million human beings—they were subhuman, they were inhu-man, they were inferior." Or, "We were just following law and order." Does that sound familiar? So it is crystal clear that self-condemnation is impossible.

And so it is with white America as a whole community. White America is incapable of condemning that which it has done to black people as a total community inside this country. There-fore we must do it, we must condemn. And after having con-demned we do not try to imitate, but begin to create. And you must understand that very, very clearly in your mind.

Sartre writes the introduction to Mr. [Frantz] Fanon's book, *The Wretched of the Earth*—he happens to be a black pragma-tist, existentialist. And Fanon says, in *The Wretched of the Earth*, of course self-condemnation is impossible. Neither of us

[4] Would this frank criticism of college fraternities and sororities tend to alienate Carmichael's audience?

can condemn ourselves and then stay alive. If we do, we become our own executioner and we must take our lives. That becomes even more important for us here in America.

Now then we come to the question of definitions. We will talk about that for a while. It is very, very important because I believe that people who can define are masters.[5]

I want to read a quote. It is one of my favorite quotes. It comes from *Alice in Wonderland* [by] Lewis Carroll. You ought to read him. Just like you ought to read *Winnie the Pooh* and *Huckleberry Finn*. Twain is my favorite author. He has got a subtlety that no other American author has been able to reach. The quote: "When I use a word," Humpty Dumpty said in a rather scornful tone, "it means just what I choose it to mean, neither more or less." "The question is," said Alice, "whether you can make words mean so many different things." "The question is," said Humpty Dumpty, "who is to be master."

That is all. That is all. Understand that. You remember a couple of years ago when our black leaders would talk about integration. They would say, "We want to integrate." They would be talking about good houses, good schools, good neighborhoods. White people would say, "You want to marry my daughter." Now you have got to understand this concept very, very clearly, because what they were doing was defining integration for these black leaders, and these black leaders allowed them to. I used to see these black leaders say, "We want to integrate." The white man would say, "You want to marry my daughter." They would say, "No, I don't want to marry your daughter. We just want to be your brother, we don't want to be your brother-in-law." Or, "We want to live next door to you, we don't want to live in your bedroom." By the time this cat finished reacting to a definition by a white man, he was out the window. And by the time he came back to be aggressive, the black community said "later" for the cat. He allowed white people to define his reaction.

Now when we get asked that question in SNCC, you know

[5] How do you interpret this statement? Is it an accurate statement?

what we say. The white woman is not the queen of the world, she is not the Virgin Mary, she can be made like any other woman.[6] Let's move on, let's move on.

Now then, that is very, very important because the same things happen. Now, I say, "black power" and someone says, "You mean violence." And they expect me to say, "No, no. I don't mean violence, I don't mean that." Later for you; I am master of my own term. If black power means violence to you, that is your problem, as is my marrying your daughter. I know what it means in my mind. I will stand clear and you must understand that because the first need of a free people is to be able to define their own terms and have those terms recognized by their oppressors. It is also the first need that all oppressors must suspend.

Camus says that when a slave says "No" he begins to exist. You see, you define to contain. That's all you do. I define this as yellow. It means that this is yellow. This is not yellow. So that when I speak of yellow you know what I am talking about. I have contained this. And so for white people to be allowed to define us by calling us Negroes, which means apathetic, lazy, stupid, and all those other things, it is for us to accept those definitions. We must define what we are and move from our definitions and tell them to recognize what we say we are.

Now you watch cowboy movies all the time. We all do. And you know there would be a fight and there would be Indians and they would be coming from the hills and Chief Crazy Horse would have a million Indians and they would be yelling, "wha, wha, wha," and they would be killing the good white women. And at last here comes the cavalry. They would come riding in and they would get out their guns and shoot up everybody— men, forward march, forward, shoot. "Look out, that one on the right." "Boom, we have got him," he's dead. They would come back and they would say, "We had a victory today. We killed the Indians." Now the next time, the Indians would beat the hell out of the white man and they would say, "Those dirty

[6] What is the likely rhetorical effect of this statement on Carmichael's audience?

Indians—they massacred us." See what they were doing. In a victory, you shoot people and you kill them that way, but in a massacre you kill them with a knife and everybody knows that's foul. Now the Indians had victories too. That we must begin to recognize. That's very important.

You ever listen to the news? Every day now, "Viet Cong terrorists today bombed and killed fifty women and children," what a shame. In the meantime, our jet bombers have been flying heavily over Hanoi, dropping bombs.

And the power to define is the most important power that we have. He is master who can define. That was made clear in the McCarthy period. If McCarthy said you were a Communist, you had to get up and say, "No, I am not a Communist." He had the power to define. It is the same thing. My fellow Americans, the Communists, the slanted-eye Viet Cong are our enemy. You must go kill them. You don't have the right to define whether or not that cat is your enemy. The master has defined it for you. And when he says "Jump," you say, "How high, boss?" So then we must begin to define our own terms and certainly our own concept of ourselves and let those who are not capable of following us fall by the wayside.[7]

Now we want to talk a little about Vietnam. We think it is drastically important. You must begin to understand the nature of this country called America, which exploits all other nonwhite countries. Now you know we are fighting for freedom, democracy, for peace. Nobody questions it. Yes, we are going to kill for freedom, democracy, and peace. Those little Chinese, Vietnamese yellow people ain't got sense enough to know they want their democracy; we are going to fight for them, give it to them because Santa Claus is still alive.[8]

I want to read a quote made August 4, 1954, before the United States governors in Seattle. Incidentally, I highly recommend this book. It is called *Vietnam, Vietnam,* by Felix Greene.

[7] Carmichael has devoted a considerable part of his speech to this matter of definition. Considering his audience, do you think he has spent a disproportionate amount of time on this matter?

[8] What rhetorical device is Carmichael using here, and how effective is it?

(Incidentally, I think the trouble with our black students is that they just don't read too much. If we could get the bougaloo like we could books, we would be up tight.) "Now let us assume," the quote says, "that we lost Indo-China." Now that is in 1953; we were not fighting the war, the French were fighting it for us. We were just giving them the money. "Now let us assume we lost Indo-China. The tin and other items we so greatly value [from that area] would cease coming." So that when the United States votes $400 million dollars to help that war, we are not voting a give-away program.

"We are after the cheapest way to prevent the occurrence of something terrible—the loss of our ability to get what we want from the riches of the Indo-Chinese territory and from Southeast Asia." That quote was made by President Dwight D. Eisenhower.

Now we may say that Dwight wasn't too smart. In our neighborhood, because he talked so well, we used to call him the white Joe Louis. But that was in 1953. So, well, we figure, you know Dwight wasn't too smart and that was a long time ago and we have become more civilized.

I want to read you a statement now, by Henry Cabot Lodge. He's the good-looking one, you know, tall, blond hair, blue eyes.[9] His quote a year ago:

Geographically, Vietnam stands at the hub of a vast area of the world, Southeast Asia. An area with a population of 249 million persons. He who holds or has influence in Vietnam can affect the future of the Philippines and Formosa to the east, Thailand and Burma with their huge rice surpluses to the west, and Malaysia and Indonesia with their rubber, ore, and tin to the south. Vietnam, thus, does not exist in a geographical vacuum from its large storehouses of wealth and the population can be influenced and undermined.

He is absolutely right. Because that's what that war is all about. And that's why we are not going. Those, then, are the words of

[9] Do these humorous *ad hominem* references to Eisenhower and Lodge add to or detract from Carmichael's persuasion?

the ambassador to Saigon. They are not my words. And he out-
lines very clearly what the war is being fought for.

If you understood anything about this country, you would
know that 75 percent of this budget is spent on war materials.
That means that for this country to survive it must always be at
war.[10] You will not get a victory for this country if you win in
Vietnam. That's no victory. The country must keep fighting.
You do not invent things that have no use. You invent them so
that they have a use. And every time you invent a better bomb,
you must drop it. So you invent another bomb. That is correct
and that is why this country keeps going at the breakneck speed
it is going in terms of its military might. And we have to understand that. Because we are told in this country that we are
civilized—another word to define.

You know Rudyard Kipling defined civilization for us. He
talked about the white man's burden. Pick up your whiteness
and go to Africa and cultivate the savages and illiterates. So
they got all these nice, white people of good will who wanted
to do well. They got in their little black robes and they went to
Africa and they saw these little black savages, man, running
around with no shirts on. "Why, you dirty man, cover up yourself. You are getting me excited." They were going to civilize
us because we were uncivilized, because we were illiterate. So
they came to Africa with the Bible and we had the land. When
they left, they had the land and we still got the Bible. And that
was civilization for them. They were civilizing us.

Indeed what is civilization? To be able to drop bombs on
Hiroshima? Is that civilization? To be able to drop bombs on
Hanoi? Is that civilization? Is it? Do we want to be civilized too?
This country has said that civilization is at stake and there is no
other solution except that of war. So what they do is, they
train us in ROTC.[11] You dig it? All they do in ROTC is teach you
how to kill. You may try to justify it all you want, but your job
is to kill. The job of the Army is to kill. That is the reason why

[10] Does the second sentence of this paragraph logically follow from the first?
[11] How appropriate is Carmichael's following discussion of ROTC to his audience? How objectionable would his position be to his audience?

it is there. Not to teach you how to become anything. If you want to be taught something, build a school in my neighborhood and let me go there. Don't tell me about going to Vietnam to learn nothing.

Now then, I have to be appalled at the president of the university who stands up and says that black power is about violence while at this very campus he encourages institutionalized violence by compulsory ROTC and does not speak about that. Who does he think he is kidding? There is nothing wrong with violence. It is just who is able to control it. That's what counts. Everybody knows that. You have institutionalized violence on your campus. You have to dress up in a monkey suit and train how to kill once a week. And what is your response to that, as black students coming to a university where they are supposed to teach you civilization? Is that civilization too? That one was killed? Is that what you are imitating? Is it for you not to reason why at a university, but to do and die? Do you not have the guts to say, "hell no"? Do you not have the guts to say: "I will not allow anyone to make me a hired killer. When I decide to kill, since it is the greatest crime that man can make, I will make that decision. And I will not only decide to kill, I will decide whom to kill."

So that you are now at a vast black university where they have already incorporated in your thinking, violence. And here you are marching around every Friday, or Thursday, or Wednesday, or whatever it is, with your shoes spit-shined 'til three o'clock in the morning, marching with a gun in your hand, learning all about how to shoot. Over in Vietnam they put you on a front line and you are shooting. But that is not violence, because you can't define for yourself. You ought to tell the school that if you wanted to learn how to kill, you would go to West Point. They turn them out there. You came here to learn how to help your people of Baltimore in the ghettos, upon whom you turn your backs as soon as you get a chance.

And what can you tell a black man in Baltimore who lives in the ghettos about killing? Hasn't he been subjected to it all of his life? What is your analysis about the rebellions that have been occurring all around the state? Are you like everybody else? Are you against violence? Do you analyze? Do you recognize what it means? Let me explain.

The reason why they say we expound violence isn't because we expound violence, but because we refuse to condemn black people who throw rocks and bottles at policemen. That is why, and I say that is the only reason why. Because I look at all the other Negro leaders—so-called leaders—every time there is a riot. "We deplore violence, we avoid use of violence, it is very, very bad, there is only a small group of vagabonds, they don't represent our community, and violence never accomplishes anything. Yes, we are training our boys to go to Vietnam. We think it is a good thing to send them to Vietnam but violence never accomplishes anything at all."

Now you have got to understand this very clearly. If you know anything about the ghetto, you would know that on any given Friday or Saturday night there is more violence inside the ghetto than any place else in any given city. You know that we cut and butcher and shoot each other. And do you also know that in any given ghetto there is more police power, that is, in terms of numbers, there are more police per block, per square inch than in any other area of the city?

What does that mean to you? It means that, on Friday night, while there are more police, there is more violence among black people. So obviously they don't give a damn about the violence among black people. . . . But one black boy throws one rock at some filthy grocery store and the whole damned National Guard comes into our ghetto. Why is that? Because property rights means more than human rights and in the ghetto we do not own the property. If we get robbed, you can call the policemen 'til you turn white. He ain't coming. But just hit a grocery store. Just throw a molotov cocktail through a window and see how quick they come in. They deplore violence. They can't stand the violence that goes on in the street. It's all right on Friday and Saturday night when we cut each other in the street and no one black man ever talks about it. We need nonviolence in the black community. That's where we need it.

We have to learn to love and respect ourselves. That's where it should begin. That's where it must begin. Because if we don't love us, ain't nobody going to love us.

Now what happens then is that the people who have power in our ghettos are the property owners. So that when their stores are touched, they call the National Guard. But to analyze that one step further, everybody in our ghettos knows that we are charged higher prices for rotten meat. Everybody knows that, but nobody says, "We deplore the high prices they charge the Negro for rotten meat." They don't say that. Nobody moves to readjust the problems black people are facing in the ghetto—the slum-lord machinery setup. And if they try to, they find out that the people who own the property are the people who make the laws.

Property rights, property rights is what the United States Constitution is based on. You should know that. . . . Property rights. People who didn't own property could not vote when this country was first founded. Not until years afterwards such people were able to vote. So the analysis is the question of property versus propertyless people. That's what it's all about.

That's what those rebellions are about. Nothing else, nothing less. And what appalls me about the black leaders is they do not have the guts to condemn the grocery-store owner. Now I will say anytime a man has been charging us all that money for fifteen years, his store should have been bombed five years ago. Should have been out of the neighborhood five years ago. And if nobody wants to do it, then you can't blame people when they move to do it for themselves. If you want to stop rebellion, then eradicate the cause.[12]

You are college students, you should think. Now then we want to talk finally about the responsibility of youth. That's black students. It is time for you to stop running away from being black. It is time for you to begin to understand that you, as the growing intellectual, the black intellectuals of this country, must begin to define beauty for black people.

Beauty in this society is defined by someone with a narrow

[12] According to Carmichael, what is the "cause" which must be eradicated?

nose, thin lips, white skin. You ain't got none of that. So now what you try to do when you pick a homecoming queen, you look for the brightest thing that looks light, bright, and damn near white. And you have your mothers sending you up here. . . . "Be sure to pick a nice-looking fellow with curly hair when you get married, dear." Or if your lips are thick, bite them in. Hold your nose; don't drink coffee because you are black.

Everybody knows black is bad. Can you begin to get the guts to develop a criteria for beauty for black people? That your nose is boss; your lips are thick, you are black, and you are beautiful? Can you begin to do it so that you are not ashamed of your hair and you don't cut it to the scalp so that naps won't show? Girls, are you ready? Obviously it is your responsibility to begin to define the criteria for black people about their beauty. Because you are running around with your Nadinola cream. Your campus, the black campuses of this country, are becoming infested with wigs and Mustangs and you are to blame for it. You are to blame for it.[13]

What is your responsibility to your fellow black brothers? Why are you here? So that you can become a social worker so that you can kick down a door in the middle of the night to look for a pair of shoes? Is that what you come to college for? So that you can keep the kid in the ghetto school, so that you can ride up in a big Bonneville with [an] AKA sign stuck on the back? Is that your responsibility? Is that your responsibility? What is your responsibility to black people of Baltimore who are hungry for the knowledge you are supposed to have?

Is it so that you can just get over? Do you forget that it is not your sweat that put you where you are? Do you not know that your black mothers scrubbed floors so you can get here, and the minute you get out, you turn your back on them? What is your responsibility, black students? What is it? Is it to become a teacher so you can be programed into a ghetto school? So that you can get up and say, "It's a shame how our children are

---

[13] In the last few paragraphs, Carmichael has been criticizing the attitudes and actions of his audience. Are these criticisms basic and to the point or rather irrelevant and unimportant to his audience?

culturally deprived"? What do you know about culturally deprived? What is your definition of culture? Isn't it anything man-made? Is it not anything man-made? How the hell can I be culturally deprived? You deny my very existence, to use that term.[14] Do you question what they tell you at school? Or do you only accept, carry it back, get over, and go out to further stymie black people in the ghetto?

I blame you for the rebellions across the country last summer. And I will blame you again when they increase more this summer. It is your obligation to be back in the ghetto helping out black people who are looking, who are acting, begging, and thinking a way to solve their problems. And you are running out of the ghetto as fast as your sports cars and Mustangs can carry you.

What is your responsibility, black students of Morgan? Do you know about DuBois? Have you read Douglass? Do you know Richard Wright? Can you quote A. J. Rogers? Do you know Claude McKay? Can you understand, can you understand LeRoi Jones?

There is a young man with me now. His name is Eldridge Cleaver. He just spent eight years in jail. He is writing some of the most profound writing that has come out in the country from black men. Do you know of him? Have you read his stuff? Why haven't you read his stuff? Is it because you are too busy trying to find out where the Kappas are partying Friday night? Why is it that you haven't read his stuff? Is it that you are spit-shining your shoes so that you can become a lieutenant colonel to go to Vietnam when you graduate? Why is it that you haven't read his stuff? Is it that you don't want to read anything about being black because you, too, are ashamed of it and are running from it? So you want to run to your debutante ball with your light-skinned girlfriend to be white. So you want to run to your Kappa fraternity ball and forget all else.

When the ghettos rebel you are going to be the buffer, and you are the ones who are going to be caught in the middle. The

[14] Why does Carmichael object to the term "culturally deprived" being applied to black Americans?

gate is swinging open. Brothers and sisters, you had better come home. You had better come home early this summer. You had better take what knowledge you have and use it to benefit black people in the ghetto. You had better recognize that individualism is a luxury that black students can no longer afford. You had better understand that. You had better begin to see yourself as a people, and as a group, and therefore you need to help to advance that group.

Can you be aggressive? Can you say that Baltimore is almost 52 percent black and black people should own, run it, lock, stock, and barrel? They do it every place else. Or, are you afraid?

Can you not go out and organize those people to take the political power which they have been denied? Can you not help? Or are you too busy trying to be a doctor and lawyer so that you can get a big car and a big house and talk about your house in the suburbs and "I'm the only one out there"?

Can you begin to say that James Brown is us, that he is a musical genius as much as Bach or Beethoven? Can you say it? Can you understand your culture? Can you make them teach it to you here in college, rather than to teach you Bach and Beethoven which is only one-sided? Why can't you also have James Brown so that you can begin to know what culture is all about?[15]

I want to finish with two quotes. The first is by Bertrand Russell. You know about the war tribunal. You should. Bertrand Russell is calling the war tribunal to judge people of this country. I want to read from what he calls "An Appeal to My Conscience" [*An Appeal to the American Conscience*]. You ought to try to understand it very clearly because what you ought to understand about the war in Vietnam is that it has interest for you not only personally, that is, during your student days, but it is very political for black people. When McNamara says he is going to draft 30 percent black people out of the ghettos, baby, that is nothing but urban removal, that's all it is. And if

[15] What differences does it make rhetorically for Carmichael to communicate attacks and criticisms against his audience in the form of questions and not in the form of declarative statements in the last few paragraphs?

you don't begin to understand that you are going to be the fellows leading the charges of your 30 percent black people. You don't understand that. Do you have the guts to stand up now and say, "I will not follow law and order, I will follow my own conscience"?

That's what they sent Eichmann to jail for, you know, because he followed law and order. And they said that there is a higher law than the law of government. There is the law of each of us and they are absolutely right. And that is my law, and I will not go to Vietnam, I will not serve in the Army. I will say, hell no. The choices are very clear. They are crystal clear. You either suffer or you inflict suffering. Either you go to Leavenworth or you become a killer. I will not become a killer. I will choose to suffer. I will go to jail. To hell with this country.

Now then the quote by Mr. Russell:

Just as in the case of Spain, Vietnam is a barbarous rehearsal. It is our intention that neither the bona fides nor the authenticity of this tribunal will be susceptible to challenge from those who have so much to hide.

President Johnson, Dean Rusk, Robert McNamara, Henry Cabot Lodge, General Westmoreland, and their fellow criminals will be brought before a wider justice than they recognize and a more profound condemnation than they are equipped to understand.

That is a profound statement.

Now the last statement that I want to leave you with is by John Donne. You know John Donne is my favorite philosophical poet of the seventeenth century. He said, "The death of any man diminishes me because I am involved in mankind."

Now what this generation has allowed to happen is that we are not involved in mankind. When we began to crawl, they sent six million people to an oven and we blinked our eyes. And when we walked, they sent our uncles to Korea. And we grew up in a cold war to continue their head-wrecking period so that we are immune to humanity. We, this generation, must save the world. We must become involved in mankind. We must not allow them to stage the killing of every and any thing that gets in their way. We must not become part of that machinery.

Now I want to read my favorite quote: "If I am not for myself, who will be? If I am for myself alone, who am I? If not now, when? And if not you, who?" [16]

I want to thank you.

STUDY QUESTIONS

1. How do you interpret Carmichael's statement that "the first need of a free people is to be able to define their own terms and have those terms recognized by their oppressors"? Do you agree that Negroes have allowed themselves to be defined by whites? Explain and give some examples to support your answer.

2. What authorities does Carmichael cite to lend support to some of his views? Are these authorities relevant to his immediate audience? How do his authorities differ from the authorities Martin Luther King cites in his "Letter from Birmingham City Jail"?

3. Are there any significant differences between the black power in this speech and the black power in the selection "Power and Racism"? Are there any similarities? Illustrate your answer with specific references to both selections.

4. What do you think Carmichael's purpose was in delivering this speech? What available means of persuasion has he used to achieve this purpose?

5. Do most of Carmichael's arguments stand up to logical analysis? Illustrate with specific passages from the speech.

6. Does the content of Carmichael's speech indicate a concern primarily with means or ends? Or both? Cite passages from the speech to support your answer.

7. Compare this speech with the speech Carmichael delivered at Mount Holyoke College on November 16, 1966; see Stokely Carmichael, "Toward Black Liberation," *Massachusetts Review*, 7 (Autumn 1966), pp. 639–651.

[16] How are the several ideas conveyed in these questions relevant to Carmichael's audience?

FLOYD B. McKISSICK

Speech at the National Conference on Black Power

JULY 21, 1967

Floyd McKissick was born March 9, 1922, in Asheville, North Carolina. He graduated from Morehouse College and the University of North Carolina Law School. He is licensed to practice law in the District of Columbia, in North Carolina, before the Federal Communications Commission, the Federal District Court of Appeals, and the United States Supreme Court as well. In 1966, Mr. McKissick was appointed national director of the Congress of Racial Equality (CORE).

Two eyes stare out of a Black Face. Kinky hair grows on a Black Head. Inside of that Black Head is a mind that is Black, forced to think Black in order to survive. To think white, to reason with the logic of a white man is only to speed the time for the Total Destruction of Black People. A Black Man cannot afford to think white: He must think Black if he is to survive.

Every day, Black People around the world see hunger, suffering, despair, disease and hatred. They see a world of oppression, presided over by a few white people dominating the masses of powerless colored people—on every continent.

Black Men have gained a special insight, an almost "privileged" perception. It is an insight acquired over years of oppression, years without freedom.

White men live in a totally different reality from Black Men.

Their thought processes are molded by experiences foreign to Black Men.[1]

Because white men cannot understand Black People or the way they feel and think—they are afraid. The white man knows that he has been the oppressor and, for that, he is guilty. His guilt makes him fear. White people without fear of Blacks are white people without guilt.[2]

White supremacy reigns in such distant and exotic places as Europe and South Africa. But the true bastion of white supremacy, that country which makes it all possible, is the United States of America.

The democratic principles taught in the United States hardly apply on a world-wide basis, for clearly the white minority controls the masses of colored and Black Peoples in the world today.

They make the rules. And the rules say that world domination is not based on democratic principles but on power.[3] There is no willingness to share that power with the colored people of the world. There is no commitment to share that power any time in the future. Yet, Black People are lost without power to bring about change.

We are given rhetoric about power sharing: "the Land of the Free. Home of the Brave." "With liberty and justice for all." I could name dozens of others that sound beautiful, but mean absolutely nothing for Black People, here or on any other continent.

They were never intended to mean anything for Black People. They were written when we were still slaves.[4]

There are Black People starving in Mississippi, millions of colored people starving in India while white Americans bask in luxury, spending millions to go to the moon, billions on a war in Vietnam which pits yellow people against yellow people.

[1] If this is true, how is it possible for members of the two races ever to understand one another? Would McKissick's audience be concerned that such understanding is "impossible"?

[2] Complete this argument by placing yourself in the second premise.

[3] Is this the same "power" Carmichael was speaking of in his "Power and Racism"?

[4] If this is true, is McKissick's conclusion that the above "slogans" were not meant originally to apply to the blacks in America?

There are rebellions throughout the United States—Black People demanding that they no longer be exploited, that they be free—free to live in dignity.

Farmers put acres of non-producing land into the federal land bank—which could feed the nation, and the world. In Mississippi, Black People starve.

The Black and colored masses are regarded merely as chattel —with a difference. We are mere consumers. And by our consumption of the goods and services of this nation—this economic, political system, we furnish the margin of profit on which the system survives.

The system of white supremacy and its manipulators are dedicated to the proposition that the system must be maintained at all cost—even at the expense of Total Destruction of Black and colored peoples in the United States and around the world—that system which exploits, denies, debases and destroys —destroys humanity, values, morality and non-white cultures.

The cry of the racist white man is: "Threaten not our system, or you will be annihilated by our National Rifle Association, the Ku Klux Klan, the White Citizens' Councils—which we fund; by the Minute Men, Birchers and vigilantes, who we condone; and by our National Guard, which is integrated, our State Militia, our State, City and County Police Forces, which are also integrated. The system of exploitation is far more important—far more precious—than human lives."

You ask: Would America intentionally starve Black People in Mississippi, feed Indians only if they agreed to domination by white people? Would America allow thousands of Blacks to be wasted on the streets of Newark or Buffalo, Watts or Atlanta, because they simply said: "Take your foot off our necks"?

Would America destroy the lives of millions of Blacks whose forebearers, as slaves, made and developed this economic— political system, by their blood, sweat and free labor? Is there not a word called Respect—another world called Mercy— another, Justice?

Many Jews in Germany thought so. During Hitler's regime, they discovered differently.

Would America systematically destroy 22 million Blacks? My answer is: Look at the record! More specifically, I believe they can. I believe they will.[5]

White supremacy stems from an inferiority complex, so does fear. The kind of fear experienced by the racist white man. The Man has no logic when dealing with Blacks. For he insists that he is superior.

He is neurotic when threatened, psychotic when confronted with truth. He cannot comprehend your needs or just demands —he cannot recognize his responsibility. He will not acknowledge his guilt or the guilt of his brothers.

Has he punished his white brothers for the civil rights murders of Blacks (or even the whites who were with us), on the highways of Mississippi, Alabama, Georgia, and throughout the south?

I regretfully advise that The Man has not, moreover, he has not even found the criminals, in many instances. But he can find, shoot and kill a sixteen year old Black Kid who loots because he doesn't have money to buy a transistor radio.[6]

Yes—The Man has the capacity to neglect, to destroy, to shoot, to kill—if his victim is not white. He has the capacity for genocide.

Until recently, genocide was a relatively unknown word. After World War II, however, it came into pretty common usage. It means: "The use or user of deliberate, systematic measures for the extermination of a racial, political or cultural group of people." It means mass murder.

In America, we are inclined to reserve this distasteful word for the planned extermination of Jews by Hitler in Nazi Germany. This is naive. Hitler's program of genocide, to be sure, is the only one we know of that was blatant enough to herd millions of people into ovens all at one time—uncouth enough to pile thousands of bodies together in one place and impolitic

[5] Does what follows persuasively establish that white America can and will "systematically destroy 22 million Blacks"?

[6] Here, and later in the speech, McKissick refers to white America's dual standard of justice, one for whites and one for blacks. Does the evidence indicate that McKissick is right?

enough to be implicit in the statement of its goals—the goal being the "Final Solution," the elimination of the Jewish People.

But one must be reminded that genocide exists in many forms and has existed throughout history. To understand the sinister nature of genocide, one must understand not only European history, but American history as well.

No, genocide is not a simple matter. It cannot just happen. One group of people cannot just go ahead and wipe out another group of people. They must first pass through several stages— they must live out a peculiar and deadly pattern.

The first prerequisite for a nation capable of genocide is the belief that they are superior to their victims. They must believe that they are entitled to the control of the life and death of their victims.

During Hitler's regime, the Germans were supplied with elaborate charts and complicated theses, supposedly proving the superiority of the German people. It is interesting to note that, at the bottom of these charts were the colored people of the world, most conspicuously, the Black People.

Until recently, in America, there were many respected scientists and anthropologists who advanced the theory that caucasians were genetically superior to colored peoples. Although in some parts of the United States, particularly in the south, the belief in genetic superiority still prevails, in the more "enlightened" areas of the North, the popular theory is that colored people, particularly Black People, are not genetically inferior. They are just inferior.

If they were not inferior, they would be better educated, live in better homes and on cleaner streets. If they were really equal, they would improve their own conditions.

In America, as we have seen, the belief in white superiority runs deep. It was a dominant factor in the slave trade. The Black African wasn't recognized as a human being.

A belief ferocious enough to allow human slavery cannot be dissipated by a mere century and, in America, it has been quietly reinforced.

Although slavery as a recognized legal institution has been

abolished, economic slavery, economic exploitation, has not. Black People in this country have never been allowed to share in the economic riches of America. A few get in—here and there—a few get rich, but their success has no effect on the masses of Black People.

White landlords, white storekeepers, white corporate managers and a white, Anglo-Saxon Wall Street, conspire to keep the Black Man in his place.

As whites quietly exit to the comfortable suburbs, they do not relinquish the economic control of the ghetto; they maintain control of the city agencies and the political scene. They determine what opportunities will be available and what will be reserved for whites only—and, occasionally, one or two good "Negroes."

With the climate existing in the United States, we would be foolish, as leaders, to think that Black People are not being politically oppressed. If Black People got political power, they might be able to merge their values with the values of the dominant culture. And the white man wants to protect his values—particularly his economic values: the materialism which has distorted his dealings with the entire world.

Their laws are used as the tools of racism. Ethics are adopted and discarded at the whim of a racist Congress. Adam Clayton Powell loses his seat in the House of Representatives for alleged offenses far less serious than those of Senator Dodd, who was merely censured for his crimes.

The offenses of which Powell was accused were less than Dodd's—but his punishment was far greater. Congress was not satisfied merely to punish Adam; they punished all the Black People of Harlem. They stripped Harlem of representation.

They made the decision to throw Adam out in less than a day of debate. It took the Senate weeks to even vote to censure Dodd.

One thing they couldn't do—they couldn't get Adam to beg. They couldn't get Our Man to come whimpering—the way they did with Thomas Dodd.

But they will keep on trying. They will organize special investigations to determine if Adam is guilty of civil offenses—while Senator Eastland, of Mississippi, is immune to even the inconvenience of defending himself against the civil charge of "conspiracy to violate civil rights in Louisiana."

These attacks upon Black Men are not restricted to economic and political means. In Newark, of 26 dead, in the recent rebellion, 24 were Black People. The ratio was similar in Watts. Not one white man died in Harlem's rebellion.

And who is to blame for the rebellions? This point we need not argue. The white man is the judge, jury and the executioner in his system and he first made the law so as to control us. We are called the violators of his "Law and Order"—"Criminals."

Yet he knows that the white racist society is to blame for all of the conditions which force a man to rebel. His concept of "Law and Order" means the legal methods of exploiting Blacks. We object and we resist.

Some so-called [7] Negro leaders even have the audacity to join The Man—by calling a Liberation Struggle a riot—his brothers hoodlums and criminals—and damning his brothers who seek to overthrow the yoke of oppression.

And when these rebellions temporarily subside—what happens? Black People are stranded without food, medical supplies and other essentials. Old people, babies, pregnant women must stand in line for hours to get one quart of rancid milk and a box of cereal.

No National Agencies come to their aid: They are left to their own devices.

We sent an urgent telegram to the President of the United States—requesting that sections of Newark be declared a National Disaster Area—so that the Red Cross and government agencies could move in with food and supplies. In response, from the Office of Emergency Planning, we received a terse message.

I quote: "Your request for the designation of the area of Newark, New Jersey as National Disaster Area has been referred

[7] Why does McKissick speak of "so-called Negro leaders"? "The Man"? Why does he object to the term "riot"?

to this office for response. Disasters are defined by this office to include only natural disasters. Therefore do not cover the circumstances of the disaster of riots in Newark."

As history unfolds, it becomes more and more apparent that questions must be raised—the same questions which were raised by the events in Nazi Germany. This time, answers must be found.

Why didn't the Jews organize to oppose Hitler? Why weren't they a solid enough political force to prevent his ascent to power? Why did so many people march so slowly to their deaths? Why didn't they resist? What techniques did the Germans apply? What methods did they use? Were not the Jews psychologically prepared for genocide? [8]

Before the mass extermination began, Jews were degraded systematically. They were confined to ghettos. They were kept apart. They were forced to wear a special badge of dishonor—the Star of David.

In America, the special badge does not need to be sewn on a man's jacket. He is always Black.

In this country, the ghetto is not defined by barbed wire: The ghetto follows the Black Man wherever he goes.

Hitler was faced with the task of destroying Jewish economic power. In America, the task is easier. The Black Man has no economic power. At this late date, there is little need to escalate economic oppression. The Black Man is at the bottom of the ladder.

Black People have always lived under fear of torture and death by this racist system—fear of being beaten by whips or chains in slavery, fear of expressing themselves at the cost of death, fear of life itself. Fear of exercising the basic rights supposedly guaranteed by the Constitution of the United States.

But we paid our dues for being a man—a slave—for seeking to express ourselves, for telling the truth about this wretched system. In slavery, they cut our heel strings to stop us from running and joining the underground railroad. Yes, we've paid our dues. It is estimated that sixty million of us died as a direct result of

[8] How meaningful and relevant are these questions to McKissick's audience?

the slave trade. They lynched us by the hundreds and thousands for simply saying what we saw.

We pay our dues today—the death penalty is primarily reserved for Blacks when a crime is committed—or alleged. "Equal Justice Under Law" is a farce when an all-white jury convicts Muhammad Ali in less than twenty minutes, when Black Men are shot in religious worship in Los Angeles because they are Muslims—when Black Leaders are afraid to speak out because, if they do, it means economic isolation.

Yes, Black People know fear and live with it each and every day of their lives—in deadly fear of the white man's potential.[9] We know he can kill, we know he will—because of his hurt pride—we know that his personality demands that he control whatever he sees, we know that normal dissent is treason in his blue eyes.

In fact, we know The Man better than he knows himself. We know him for what he is. We know he will kill us if he can— one by one or all at once.

Yet, in spite of all this, there are those of us who have been defeated by his tactics, misled by his propaganda machine.

It is evident that too many American Black People are psychologically prepared for genocide. Too many Black People believe that they are really inferior. Too many Black People want to look like the white man and be like the white man.

Hitler's propaganda techniques have been refined and expanded. The propaganda of white supremacy is advanced through advertising, entertainment and through education and folklore that ignores the contributions of Black People to World Civilization; through the acceptance of the European standard of beauty and culture, while disparaging and disregarding the values of three quarters of the world—while ignoring the beauty that is Black.

How else could you explain the failure of some Black People to understand and accept Black Power? Any rational person or group of people understand the need for self-preservation.

[9] Has McKissick persuasively conveyed the background for this fear? Can whites in any way know this fear? Can whites understand it?

Could it be that some Black People have been so misled, so confused by white America that they don't understand they need power of their own to protect themselves? Could it be that some middle-class Negroes have become so enamored with the death-wish of integration—the dream of absorption and disappearance into the white man's culture—that he fears his Blackness?

Maybe it's that too few Black People are aware of the machinery already set up for their possible destruction. Maybe they don't know about the McCarran Act.

Title II of the McCarran Act provides the Attorney General with the power in the event of an "Internal Security Emergency," to apprehend and detain "all persons as to whom there is reasonable ground to believe that such person probably will engage in or probably will conspire with others to engage in espionage or sabotage."

Maybe Black People don't think that the American government, that an American Attorney General, would ever utilize such a power. But, remember during World War II, those concentration camps were used for the internment of Japanese-Americans. The property of many innocent yellow people was confiscated. To this day, fair reparations have never been paid.

Maybe Black People feel that it is more important to be American than to be Black. Many Jews in Nazi Germany mistakenly felt it was more important to be a German than to be a Jew. Those who survived know better now.

The government could, and would, use almost any excuse to declare an Internal Security Emergency.

Opposition to the War in Vietnam, the constitutional exercise of the right to dissent, has already been equated with disloyalty and treason. General Westmoreland was brought all the way back from the battlefields of Vietnam to merge dissent with disloyalty in the minds of the American people. Such pronouncements by the Commander of the American Armed Forces can only feed an atmosphere of hysteria about the war which could be used to justify the use of Title II.

We are experiencing another Long, Hot Summer. We are faced with violence in our cities and on our campuses. These rebellions against an oppressive system, these outbursts of frustration and hopelessness, could also be used to justify the use of Title II.

The white man has never pulled any stops in his drive for advancement. When he decided that he wanted land—rich American land—not one thought was given to the systematic slaughter of American Indians. In 1600, there were about 589,000 Indians on this continent. Over 200,000 of those people belonged to tribal groups which are now extinct.

Extinct. That means that whole tribes, whole groups of people, were wiped out. More than 60 percent of the entire Indian population was exterminated. Those who lived, were herded onto reservations.

Those Indians were victims of the white man's drive for the control of land. Land has always been the tap root of the capitalist system: Land is wealth and the use of land controls the people—both physically and mentally.

An example of this, in 1967, is the Urban Renewal Act. This act, which was supposed to be designed to provide low cost housing, has never been used for that purpose. Urban Renewal has helped eliminate Black Ownership of property. It has been used to destroy the potential for the development of Black Political Power by the scattering of Black Citizens. In fact, it has been "Negro Removal."

When the Black People are removed, the land is transferred over to businessmen for redevelopment purposes, re-zoned and given an increased value. It is almost always used for middle income housing. In any event, the Black People are not able to return.

Genocide is a political decision. It can be made by a town, city, state, nation or group of nations. It was a political decision, for example, to exterminate the Communists in Indonesia. It was a political decision for the CIA to engineer the coup.

The London *Times* estimated the dead at nearly one million in the period of four months—five times as many people died in Indonesia as in Vietnam in twelve years.

The techniques and tactics of genocide vary. The prevalent

pattern has been, in recent years—to engineer coups where it is rumored that the Communists might take over.

In these cases, they have been successful in getting right wing Indonesians to fight left wing Indonesians, South Vietnamese to fight North Vietnamese, South Koreans to fight North Koreans and, in the Congo, Ghana, and other parts of Africa —to deliberately raise issues which result in tribal warfare.

In this way, the white man keeps his hands clean and he is able to obtain the spoils of bloody civil wars. For he is, in fact, the only beneficiary.

It will be interesting to watch what will happen in the near future in such places as Thailand, Cambodia and Laos.

We cannot let those patterns which have already been applied so successfully around the world and which are already in motion in this country—be carried to their logical, ultimate conclusion. These patterns must be halted now.

And we must be the ones to do it. We cannot expect help from anyone but ourselves.

Even our friends in the peace movement find it too easy to look thousands of miles away from home and, with much indignation, see the extermination of the Vietnamese.

On the other hand, they cannot see ten blocks away, where many Black People are the Walking Dead—dead in mind and spirit, because of lack of hope and lack of chance.

We cannot look elsewhere for help. We cannot lean on the crutch of religion. We cannot depend on phony "coalitions." We must work out our own methods. We must draw our own conclusions.

To those queasy individuals who are afraid of the resolutions presented here, let me state my unequivocal opinion: The right of revolution is a constitutional right, condoned by the creation of the American Constitution itself. When we assert the right of revolution, we are asserting a constitutional right.

Revolution in America is justified by all standards of morality—religious and ethical: It is required to fulfill the basic, natural rights of man.

Even white men recognized the need for revolution when, in

1776, they revolted because they were oppressed. And today—1967—Black People are more oppressed than any white man has ever been—in the history of the world.[10]

This is the time when we must unite—Brothers and Sisters. We must join in making plans.

The Congress of Racial Equality (CORE) has some ideas for programs in this regard—some short range and some long range. We are a common front into which all Black People can unite.[11]

There is a need for a Black Brain Trust. Black People with the best minds in the country must come together to help organize and plan strategy for our future, to plan for every aspect of our existence—political, economic, cultural—international.

This is not a problem of Civil Rights—it is a problem of Black Survival. The concept of civil rights is pitifully insignificant when our very lives are at stake.

A Black Fund-Raising Base must be established. As long as the white man controls the purse strings, he will hold them tightly around our necks.

We must develop second line leadership in all-Black organizations. We must develop training programs throughout this country.

We must develop effective, sophisticated security systems —a national system of communication.

We must oppose the War in Vietnam but, more important, we must educate Black Youth not to participate in that war— now.

We must develop ways and means of dealing with those "Negroes" who sell us out—who betray their people.

We see the need to develop a Black Political Base. When an incompetent like Hugh Addonizio runs a city like Newark— where over 60 percent of the population is Black—we need our own political base.

Addonizio had advance warning of what would happen in his community. But Hughie insisted that race relations in Newark

[10] How persuasive is this argument related to the colonists' revolution?
[11] Which of the several proposals made by McKissick in the following paragraphs would be unacceptable to whites? To blacks?

were good. According to the *U. S. News and World Report* of May 23, 1966, Addonizio said: "We haven't had any racial difficulties in Newark so far, and we don't anticipate any in the future. I think it's wrong for people to go around making statements like that. They could stir up the trouble we're trying so hard to avoid."

Those don't sound like the words of a man who understands the Black Community.

Then, to further illustrate his contempt for the Black Community, Hughie goes to appoint a white political hack with a high school education for the important and responsible job of Secretary of the Board of Education.

The Black Community demanded that Wilbur Parker, City Budget Director, a Certified Public Accountant with a Master's degree, be appointed. And to avoid doing that—to avoid his responsibility to Black People—Hughie convinced the present Secretary to remain.

But that is only one incident, only a tiny phase of a career of contempt, of disrespect.

In Newark, and in all cities where Black People are in the majority, the administration must be responsive to the needs of the people—must respect the demands of the Black Community. In any community where more than 60 percent of the people are Black—we need a Black Mayor.

In fact, the question of a white man's competency becomes irrelevant when a city is more than 60 percent Black. If he's white, he shouldn't be Mayor.[12]

There comes a time in the relations between a people and an elected official that the people must say: "Enough!"

That time has arrived in Newark. The people must exercise their undeniable right to clean house. Too long, white elected officials have in these United States . . . been immune from the wrath of the Black Population. They have translated this immunity into an utter disregard for the rights and prerogatives of Black People.

[12] How can this position of government by color be justified?

Black People must eliminate these evils: There is no better place to start than Newark.

We have consulted with the progressive Black Leaders of this community. It is agreed that there must be a Recall Election to get rid of Hugh Addonizio and replace him with a Black Mayor.

This conference should go on record at this time in support of the citizens of Newark in a recall election.

CORE is appointing Bob Curvin and James Hooper of the Congress of Racial Equality in Newark to spearhead and join in with other groups and individuals, to organize and coordinate this effort. Your assistance will be desperately needed.

People will be needed—volunteers who are willing to work—willing to get thousands of signatures on petitions to recall Addonizio.

The recall effort must be followed up with a Black Conference for the purpose of selecting one Black Candidate, who will be Newark's next mayor; for the purpose of organizing a Black Voter Registration Campaign Committee; for the purpose of organizing a Newark Black Candidates Fund Committee—for the purpose of making Black Political Power in Newark a reality.

As men, we must now stand up. If we are truly men and believe what we say, and live by our convictions—we must be steadfast. Men are known not by words, but by deeds—and men we must be.[13]

STUDY QUESTIONS

1. Keeping in mind McKissick's immediate audience, how would you judge his audience adaptation? What is McKissick's purpose in this speech?

2. What similarities and differences are there between the content of McKissick's speech and the content of Carmichael's speech? What are the differences between McKissick's and Wilkins' programs for alleviating the plight of the Negro? Whose program seems more effective? Explain.

[13] If it is true, as suggested by psychologists and sociologists, that the black American community has been primarily a matriarchal society, how important an appeal is this to McKissick's audience?

3. What evidence does McKissick present to demonstrate that white Americans are not above sending Negroes to concentration camps and not above practicing genocide?

4. What statements and ideas in McKissick's speech do you find hard to accept? Explain.

5. Do you detect any fallacious arguments in McKissick's speech? If so, where?

6. To what emotions does McKissick appeal? Illustrate with references to specific passages. How do these emotional appeals differ from those used by Martin Luther King in his "Letter from Birmingham City Jail"?

7. An interview with Floyd McKissick appears in *U. S. News and World Report*, 60 (May 23, 1966), pp. 40–42. Why, according to McKissick, have some Negroes turned away from nonviolence and toward violence as a means of achieving their aims? What does he suggest as a remedy for this violence?

8. See Lerone Bennett, Jr., "What's in a Name? Negro vs. Afro-American vs. Black," *Ebony*, 23 (November 1967), pp. 46–54, for a discussion on the significance of the relationship between language and Negro identity. Is the conclusion of the article that things can be changed by changing names? Is it important whether we use the term "Negro," or "black," or "Afro-American"?